English Skills 5

Answers

Carol Matchett

Schofield & Sims

WHICH BOOK?

The **English Skills** books are aligned with the end-of-year objectives for Key Stage 2. For the majority of pupils aged 7 to 11, follow the guidance given on page 2 as to which book to use with each year group.

If a pupil is working significantly above or below the standard normally expected for his or her age, another book may be more appropriate. If you are not sure which to choose, two simple **Entry tests** are available to help you identify the book that is best suited to the pupil's abilities. You can also use these resources with new pupils joining your class or school.

Photocopy masters of the **Entry tests** are provided in the teacher's guide – which also contains the **Entry test marking keys**, full instructions for use, and a range of other **English Skills** copymasters, including **Diagnostic checks**, which help to identify topics that pupils may be struggling with. The **Diagnostic check marking keys** provide catch-up activities for each topic, in the form of activity prompts, to help secure pupils' knowledge. For ordering details, see page 46.

You may be using **English Skills** at Key Stage 3 or with other mixed-ability groups of young people or adults. In such cases you will find the **Entry tests** vital in deciding which book to give each student.

Published by **Schofield & Sims Ltd**, Dogley Mill, Fenay Bridge, Huddersfield HD8 0NQ, UK
Telephone 01484 607080
www.schofieldandsims.co.uk

This edition copyright © Schofield & Sims Ltd, 2017
First edition published in 2011

Author: **Carol Matchett**
Carol Matchett has asserted her moral right under the Copyright, Designs and Patents Act, 1988, to be identified as the author of this work.

British Library Cataloguing in Publication Data
A catalogue record for this book is available from the British Library.

Design by **Ledgard Jepson Ltd**
Front cover design by **Peter Grundy**
Printed in the UK by **Page Bros (Norwich) Ltd**

ISBN 978 07217 1413 4

CONTENTS

Introduction

Schofield & Sims English Skills provides regular and carefully graded practice in key literacy skills. It is designed for use alongside your existing English lessons, embedding key aspects of grammar, sentence structure, punctuation and spelling and constantly revisiting them until they become automatic. At the same time, it reinforces and develops pupils' knowledge of word structure and vocabulary.

Each pupil book comprises three sections with 12 tests in each one. The tests become more difficult, but the increase in difficulty is gradual. The pupil books are fully compatible with the Key Stage 2 National Curriculum, and the final tests in each book are aligned with the end-of-year objectives as follows:

- **Introductory Book:** Years 1 and 2 (Bridge to lower KS2)
- **Book 1:** Year 3
- **Book 2:** Year 4
- **Book 3:** Years 4 and 5 (Bridge to upper KS2)
- **Book 4:** Year 5
- **Book 5:** Year 6
- **Book 6:** Years 6 and 7 (Bridge to KS3)

Parts A, B and C

Each test is divided into three parts:

- Part A: **Warm-up** – puzzles, 'warm-up' exercises and revision of earlier learning
- Part B: **Word work** – spelling, word structure, exploring words and their meanings to help develop vocabulary
- Part C: **Sentence work** – constructing and punctuating sentences; using words from different word classes; understanding tense, verb forms and other aspects of grammar.

Answering the test questions

After you have demonstrated to the class how some of the different question types are to be answered, the pupils work through the test items without adult help – either individually or in pairs. Encourage them to refer to dictionaries, thesauruses and other appropriate reference materials rather than asking for your help. The tests may be used flexibly. For example, a test may be tackled in one session or over several days.

Marking

This book provides correct answers for **English Skills 5**; where various different answers would be acceptable, an example is provided. The **Focus** panel stating the areas of learning being tested helps you to decide whether the pupil's answer is satisfactory. **Please note and explain to the class that if all or part of a question has several possible answers, the question number is displayed like this ⑤. If a question has a specific answer, the question number is displayed like this ⑤. It is displayed in this way even if the answer is made up of several parts that may be given in any order.**

Some questions test more than one area: for example, a question on writing in the past tense might also check pupils' knowledge of the spelling rules for adding **ed**. In such cases, both parts of the answer must be correct, reflecting real-life situations that require varied knowledge and skills.

Group marking sessions

Some teachers find that group or class marking sessions led by the teacher or classroom assistant are the most effective way of marking the tests: pupils learn by comparing and discussing answers.

Another benefit of group or class marking sessions is that they quickly highlight gaps in pupils' knowledge, which will help to inform your future teaching. Where pupils have given a wrong answer, or none at all, briefly reinforce the key teaching point using an item from this book as a model. At the end of the session, encourage pupils to evaluate their own successes and identify what they need to remember next time or when they are writing.

Suggested questions to ask in a marking session:
- What was this question testing?
- How many different 'correct' answers did we come up with?
- Were some sentence or word choices more interesting or effective than others? Why?
- How do we know this answer is correct?
- How can we make the answer correct?
- Is there an answer that would be even better?
- What are the key points to remember next time?
- When might we put these key points into practice in our reading or writing?

Marking the end-of-section assessments

At the end of each section are two writing assessments: the **Writing task** and the **Proofreading task**. These check that pupils are applying in their writing the knowledge, skills and understanding developed in the weekly tests. The assessments also provide evidence of a pupil's strengths and weaknesses, which will help you to set appropriate targets. You might consider sharing with the pupils a simplified version of the mark scheme – and then involve them in setting their own targets for improving their writing.

• *The writing task*

The **Writing task** helps you assess a pupil's written composition. Prompts help pupils to plan and gather ideas so that when they begin writing they can focus on selecting appropriate grammar, vocabulary and sentence structures to express their ideas clearly and effectively. On pages 16, 30 and 44 you will find photocopiable **Writing task assessment sheets** – one for each section – with specific assessment points arranged under the headings 'Sentence structure and punctuation', 'Composition and effect' and 'Spelling'. Complete one of these sheets as you mark each pupil's work.

• *The proofreading task*

The **Proofreading task** focuses on correcting punctuation, grammar and spelling. Examples of **Completed proofreading tasks** for each section, also photocopiable, are supplied on pages 17, 31 and 45. However, please note that pupils may choose to correct some of the errors using methods different to those shown in the example, but which are equally valid. For example, two main clauses might be joined using a conjunction or separated to make two sentences. Additional evidence gained from the relevant **Proofreading task** will help you to further assess pupils' achievements in 'Sentence punctuation' and 'Spelling' as already assessed in the **Writing task**. If you wish, you can use the photocopiable sheet to make notes on a pupil's work.

Please note: Where the assessment statements reveal weaknesses in a pupil's writing, work with the pupil to identify areas to develop and set targets for future writing. All the books revisit difficult areas so there will also be more opportunities for further practice.

Progress chart

On page 46 of the pupil book you will find a **Progress chart**, with one column each for Sections 1, 2 and 3, and a list of 'I can' statements relating to the kinds of activities practised in the section. Please ask every pupil to complete the relevant column when they have finished working through a section.

The **Progress chart** encourages pupils to monitor their own work by identifying those activities that they have mastered and those requiring further attention. When pupils colour in the chart as recommended (green for easy, orange for getting there and red for difficult), it gives a clear picture of progress. It also shows the benefits of systematic practice: an activity that the pupil cannot perform in Section 1 later gets the 'green light'.

The **Progress chart** promotes self-assessment and personalised learning. However, you may also wish to make a copy for your own record-keeping. For this reason, it may be photocopied.

A Warm-up

Write a sentence about computers.

1 In the past, *people mainly used computers at work.*

2 Today, *most people have computers at home.*

3 In the future, *children might have all their lessons on computers.*

Underline the word that is **not** correct.

4 decide recent <u>recide</u> recite decent

5 sacrifice menace advice <u>reverce</u> reduce

Write the antonym.

6 **inferior** *superior*

7 **backhand** *forehand*

8 **minor** *major*

9 **exterior** *interior*

10 **expansion** *contraction*

PART A Focus
1–3: linking adverbials;
past, present, future time
4–5: s sound spelt c
6–10: antonyms

B Word work

1 Add the missing letters.

PART B Focus
1–2: spelling patterns;
plural rules
3–6: unstressed endings
er, or
7–10: words with two
meanings; word classes

i e y

v a r **i** e t y   m **y** s t e r y

2 Write the plural forms of both words.

varieties   *mysteries*

3 Add the suffix **er** or **or**.

perform *er*   **invent** *or*   **collect** *or*

4 Describe the words you have created.

Nouns naming people who carry out particular activities.

Write three more words of this type.

5 **ending er** *voyager, manager, jogger*

6 **ending or** *creator, sailor, doctor*

Write different definitions of each word.

7 **hamper** (verb) *to stop or slow progress*

8 **hamper** (noun) *large basket for picnic food*

9 **coast** (verb) *to cruise along*

10 **coast** (noun) *where land meets sea*

C Sentence work

Add a preposition phrase to the start of the sentence.

PART C Focus
1–4: preposition phrases at the
start of a sentence; commas
after fronted adverbials
5–7: formal vocabulary
8–10: punctuating direct speech

1 *In the tunnel,*   it was completely dark.

2 *By seven o'clock,*   it was completely dark.

3 *At the edge of the forest,*   the man turned and spoke.

4 *Without warning,*   the man turned and spoke.

Write more formal verbs that could replace the underlined words.

5 The RSPCA <u>asked</u> people to <u>help</u> as it <u>tried</u> to <u>cope with</u> the crisis. *urged, assist, struggled, manage*

6 Residents <u>left</u> the meeting, <u>saying</u> that the situation had not been <u>sorted</u>.

departed, declaring, resolved

7 If you <u>want</u> further information, <u>go to</u> the website where you can <u>find out</u> more.

require, visit, discover

Add punctuation and capital letters to these examples of direct speech.

8 Indira said, "It is very sad. We all feel let down."

9 "It's not fair," Mick complained. "I want to go with you."

10 "It was bitterly cold," explained Bill, "and the streets were covered with ice."

X DEFINITIVE ANSWER X SAMPLE ANSWER

A Warm-up

Continue the sentence after the subordinating conjunction.

1. He stayed with Jen until *help came.*

2. He stayed with Jen as long as *he dared.*

Write four words formed by adding a prefix or suffix to the word **port**.

3. *transport*   5. *portable*

4. *porter*   6. *portal*

7. Add the same suffix to both words to make them into adjectives.

   excuse *able*   **charge** *able*

8. Add a different prefix to each of the words you have made. Write the new words.

   inexcusable, rechargeable

Write a synonym for the word in **bold**.

> **PART A Focus**
> **1–2:** using a range of conjunctions
> **3–6:** building words from root words
> **7–8:** able; prefixes
> **9–10:** synonyms

9. **persuade** *convince*

10. **discuss** *debate*

B Word work

Underline the word that is spelt correctly.

1. <u>dependent</u> observent
2. innocant <u>tolerant</u>
3. <u>convenient</u> ignorent
4. <u>expectant</u> obediant

> **PART B Focus**
> **1–5:** words ending ant, ent
> **6–7:** words ending tion, sion, ssion, cian; suffixes to change word class
> **8–10:** formal and informal synonyms

5. Write the correct spellings of the words that were wrongly spelt.

   observant, innocent, ignorant, obedient

6. Add the correct spelling of the ending that sounds like 'shun'.

   techni *cian*   **comple** *tion*

   profe *ssion*   **conclu** *sion*

7. What kind of words have you made by adding the suffixes? Underline the correct answer.

   verbs <u>nouns</u> adjectives

Write two more formal synonyms of the words in **bold**.

8. I'm **whacked**.   *exhausted, drained*

9. It's a **phoney**.   *fake, forgery*

10. We must **come clean**.   *confess, admit it*

C Sentence work

Combine the two sentences by using a relative clause.

> **PART C Focus**
> **1–3:** combining sentences; using relative clauses
> **4–6:** identifying uses of adverbs, including possibility
> **7–10:** the possessive apostrophe with plurals

1. A theatre is a public building. Plays are performed there.

   A theatre is a public building where plays are performed.

2. An orchestra is a group of musicians. They play many kinds of instruments.

   An orchestra is a group of musicians who play many kinds of instruments.

3. A thermostat is a device on a heater. It controls the temperature.

   A thermostat is a device on a heater that controls the temperature.

Underline the adverb and explain why the writer has used it.

4. <u>Perhaps</u> she could have helped me. *It shows that it is a possibility, not certain.*

5. He is <u>very</u> clever. *It intensifies the adjective.*

6. <u>Unfortunately</u>, City won 2–0. *It shows the writer's view of the events.*

Complete the phrase by writing in an item or items belonging to the characters. Use the correct punctuation.

7. **the pirates'** *treasure*

8. **the witches'** *cauldron*

9. **the gang**'s *hideaway*

10. **the sheep**'s *pen*

X **DEFINITIVE ANSWER**   X **SAMPLE ANSWER**

SECTION 1 | Test 3

A Warm-up

Continue the sentence with two preposition phrases.

1   Anil was left there *in the field for nearly an hour.*

2   Anil was left there *throughout the night without any food.*

3   Anil was left there *on his own with his dog for company.*

4   Continue the sentence using a conjunction.
    Anil was left there *while the others searched the garden.*

Add the same prefix to make three words.

5   **uni** son   **uni** corn   **uni** cycle

6   **inter** cept   **inter** rupt   **inter** sect

7   **super** nova   **super** highway   **super** power

Add the missing letters.

8   r h *y* t h m

9   a w k w *a* r d

10 q u *e* u e

> **PART A Focus**
> **1–4:** sentences using preposition phrases; conjunctions
> **5–7:** prefixes
> **8–10:** words that are often misspelt

B Word work

The same syllable is missing from both words.
Write it in.

1   wid *en* ing   threat *en* ing

2   mis *er* able   gen *er* ous

3   con *fer* ence   re *fer* ence

Split the word to show the root word, prefix and suffix.

4   unachievable   *un* / *achieve* / *able*

5   regeneration   *re* / *generate* / *tion*

6   unbeneficial   *un* / *benefit* / *(c)ial*

Add a prefix and a suffix to make an adjective.

7   *un* control *lable*

8   *in* destruct *ible*

> **PART B Focus**
> **1–3:** unstressed syllables
> **4–6:** root words; prefixes and suffixes
> **7–8:** forming adjectives; able, ible
> **9–10:** synonyms

Circle all the words that are synonyms of each other.

9   apply (appal) please (horrify) haul (shock)

10 calm (rash) mild (hasty) (reckless) sane

C Sentence work

Use a parenthesis to add the information from the second sentence into the first. Write the new sentence.

1   **Michael helped David to escape. Michael is David's brother.**
    Michael – David's brother – helped him to escape.

2   **Fatima raised £1000 for the charity. She works in a bank.**
    Fatima (who works in a bank) raised £1000 for the charity.

3   **Ben won first prize. He is aged sixteen.**   *Ben, aged sixteen, won first prize.*

Sort the modal verbs into two groups. **must might could can may will should shall**

4   **show certainty** *must, can, will, shall*   5   **show possibility** *might, could, may, should*

Change the sentence from a certainty to a possibility. Cross out one word and write a new one.

6   **Mr Jones said that we could ~~definitely~~ play cricket this afternoon.**   *possibly*

7   **Other people said they ~~will~~ help if needed.**   *might*

> **PART C Focus**
> **1–3:** using commas, brackets or dashes to indicate a parenthesis
> **4–7:** modal verbs to show possibility
> **8–10:** sentence punctuation; commas to mark clauses or phrases

Add the missing full stops, commas and capital letters.

8   Aaron ran down the hill, shouting loudly. The dog, ignoring me, bounded after him.

9   After two difficult years, Marie, then aged ten, went to live with her grandmother.

10 As the strangers came to a halt, Jessica looked up. Her face was pale and frightened.

X DEFINITIVE ANSWER   X SAMPLE ANSWER

A Warm-up

We spoke _____ .

Write two adverbs that could be used to show

1 **how**   nervously   briefly

2 **where**   outside   here

3 **when**   yesterday   later

Add the missing prefix.

Clue: to do with computers

4   inter **active**

5   hyper **link**

6   multi **media**

> PART A Focus
> **1–3:** use of adverbs
> **4–7:** prefixes
> **8–10:** word classes

7 Write one other word with each prefix.

    intergalactic, hypermarket, multicoloured

Underline the odd one out.

8 **possessive pronouns**   ours its his <u>there's</u>

9 **prepositions**   with at during <u>an</u>

10 **conjunctions**   but if <u>all</u> until

B Word work

Add each suffix and write the new words.

ed ment

1 **equip**   equipped, equipment

2 **commit**   committed, commitment

> PART B Focus
> **1–2:** adding suffixes
> **3:** words ending **ence**
> **4–6:** prefixes with hyphens
> **7–10:** words with more than one meaning

3 Add the same ending to both words.

    consequ ence   **influ** ence

Add two more words with the same prefix.

4 **ex-teacher**

    ex-president   ex-player

5 **semi-conscious**

    semi-detached   semi-skimmed

6 Write the meaning of the prefixes.

    semi- partly   **ex-** former

Write four different definitions.

7 **beat**   the feel of the rhythm in music

8 **beat**   to whisk with a fork in cookery

9 **beat**   to defeat

10 **beat**   to strike or hit

C Sentence work

Name the type of sentence and explain why the writer has used it in the title.

1 **Does the Loch Ness monster really exist?**   a question   It intrigues the reader.

2 **Act now to save the whale.**   a command   It tells the reader to do it.

3 **What a show!**   an exclamation   It sounds exciting.

4 Make this statement into a question. Do it in two ways.

    There is a solution.   Is there a solution?   There is a solution, isn't there?

Rewrite the sentence so that it sounds less definite.

5 **The cake will be ready on time.**   The cake should be ready on time.

6 **In the future we will all have electric cars.**   In the future we might all have electric cars.

7 **Michael used the key to escape.**   Michael may have used the key to escape.

Complete the sentence by adding a parenthesis.

8 **The team**   – all seven of them –   **played well.**

9 **The castle**   (built in 1466)   **stands on a hill.**

10 **Olivia**   , who was walking her dog,   **found the painting.**

> PART C Focus
> **1–3:** selecting sentence types for effect
> **4:** forming questions; question tags
> **5–7:** modal verbs to show possibility
> **8–10:** commas, brackets and dashes to indicate a parenthesis

A Warm-up

Use the words **cat** and **bowl** in a

1 **sentence** My cat will only eat from her bowl.

2 **command** Give the cat a bowl of cold milk.

3 **question** Where has the cat hidden its bowl?

4 **sentence with a relative clause**
   The cat found the bowl that was in the kitchen.

weary polite tidy

Add the same suffix to each of the three words to make

5 **nouns** weariness, politeness, tidiness

6 **adverbs** wearily, politely, tidily

Add the missing letters. *Clue: buildings*

7 h o s p i t a l

8 r e s t a u r a n t

9 o b s e r v a t o r y

10 g y m n a s i u m

PART A Focus
1–4: sentence types; relative clauses
5–6: suffixes; word classes
7–10: words that are often misspelt

B Word work

1 Add **ie** or **ei**.

   p ie rce   br ie fly   rec ei pt

2 What rule did you use?
   'i' before 'e' except after 'c'

3 Underline the letter string in all the words.
   <u>ough</u> tr<u>ough</u> pl<u>ough</u> thor<u>ough</u> b<u>ough</u>

4 Write the two words where the letter string makes the same sound.
   plough   bough

PART B Focus
1–2: i before e rule
3–4: letter string **ough**
5–7: root words; word families
8–10: subject-specific vocabulary

Write three words related to the root word in **bold**.

5 **hero** heroism, heroic, superhero

6 **just** justice, justly, injustice

7 **know** knowing, knowledge, known

Write a definition. *Clue: to do with plants*

8 **germination** when a seed starts sprouting

9 **dispersal** how seeds are scattered

10 **pollination** how pollen is transferred

C Sentence work

Identify the text type. Underline the longer noun phrase at the start of the sentence.

1 <u>The brave teenager</u>, now resting at home, rescued her trapped friends.   newspaper report

2 <u>Hundreds of homeless animals</u> are in urgent need of your help – right now.   persuasive text

3 <u>The man with the white beard</u> stood in the quiet, moonlit square.   story

Give two ways in which the nouns in the above phrases are modified.

4 using expressive/descriptive adjectives   5 using prepositional phrases

Write four modal verbs that could be used to complete the sentence.

6 He _____ be late today.   could, might, will, may

7 They _____ have passed us.   may, will, must, could

8 Put a tick if the apostrophes are used correctly. Put a cross if they are not.

   Jenny's mum hadn't any money.   ✓   Fan's were eager to see Citys' new signing.   ✗

   We could'nt hear the actor's dialogue.   ✗

Write correctly the sentences that you have put a cross beside.

9 We couldn't hear the actors' dialogue.

10 Fans were eager to see City's new signing.

PART C Focus
1–3: identifying text types; expanded noun phrases
4–5: noun modification
6–7: modal verbs
8–10: using apostrophes

X **DEFINITIVE ANSWER**   X **SAMPLE ANSWER**

A Warm-up

Write a sentence about a new snack called choco-pops. Begin with the given determiner.

1 **This** snack is the perfect chocolate treat.

2 **An** amazing new snack for you to try.

3 **Some** snacks are boring but choco-pops are a taste sensation.

4 **Every** bite is like a chocolate explosion on your tongue.

What word could you write in the gap to make a new word? Write two possibilities.

5 in _____ ly   sincere, correct

6 un _____ ably   avoid, comfort

7 ir _____ ibly   response, resist

Add the name of a household item to complete the word.

8 e n v iron m e n t

9 o c cup y

10 a c c o m pan y

PART A Focus
1–4: use of determiners
5–7: word structure; ly, ably, ibly
8–10: words that are often misspelt

B Word work

Cross out the words that are wrongly spelt. Write the correct spellings.

1 The ~~fourty soldures~~ were ~~incredibley~~ brave.
forty, soldiers, incredibly

2 Can ~~amatures compeat~~ with ~~prefessionels~~?
amateurs, compete, professionals

Add two words with the same suffix.

3 **quarrelsome**   troublesome, fearsome
4 **toward**   downward, onward
5 **lengthwise**   clockwise, likewise

Draw a line to match the synonyms.

6 enforce — impose
7 desert — propose
8 suggest — abandon

PART B Focus
1–2: common spelling errors
3–5: suffixes
6–8: synonyms
9–10: words with more than one meaning; word classes

Underline the words that

9 can be **nouns** as well as **adjectives**
ugly <u>annual</u> large <u>final</u> busy

10 can be **nouns** as well as **verbs**
<u>cook</u> rely <u>polish</u> deliver compose

C Sentence work

Reorder the words to make three better sentences. Start each one with a different adverbial.

The king saw the statue unfortunately as he entered the castle in the evening.

1 Unfortunately, the king saw the statue in the evening as he entered the castle.

2 As he entered the castle in the evening, unfortunately the king saw the statue.

3 In the evening, the king unfortunately saw the statue as he entered the castle.

Cross out the words that are informal. Write new words that sound more formal.

4 They ~~got rid~~ of the ~~stuff~~.   disposed, goods

5 They ~~got hold~~ of the ~~kit~~.   seized, equipment

6 The ~~bloke~~ seemed a ~~bit shady~~.   gentleman, little untrustworthy

Add a pair of brackets within each sentence.

7 Some eagles build their nests (called eyries) on cliff tops.

8 Ned kept the two dogs (Shep and Flick) for many years.

9 Rob Jones (the team's manager) was unhappy with the decision.

10 What other punctuation could have been used instead of brackets?   a pair of commas or dashes

PART C Focus
1–3: reordering phrases, clauses, adverbs; commas after fronted adverbials
4–6: formal vocabulary
7–10: commas, brackets and dashes to indicate a parenthesis

X DEFINITIVE ANSWER   X SAMPLE ANSWER

SECTION 1 | Test 7

A Warm-up

Use the words **football** and **cake** in a sentence with

1 **one clause** The football landed in
the cake.

2 **two clauses** After playing football
for an hour, we devoured the cake.

3 Join a prefix to the word to make a verb.

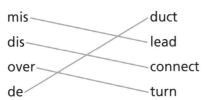

mis   duct
dis   lead
over   connect
de   turn

> **PART A Focus**
> **1–2:** single and multi-clause sentences
> **3–7:** verb prefixes
> **8–10:** compound words

Use the words to complete these phrases.

4 disconnect a cable   6 deduct points
5 overturn a boat   7 mislead people

All these compound words are to do with computers.
Complete them using

8 **adjectives** short cut   hard ware
9 **prepositions** down load   on line
10 **nouns** task bar   net work

B Word work

1 Underline the root words.

outrageous prosperous rebellious

2 Which root word changes when **ous** is added?
rebel   **because** you double the 'l'
and add 'ious'

3 Complete these word sums.

medal + ist = medallist
control + able = controllable

> **PART B Focus**
> **1–2:** spelling rules for adding ous
> **3:** adding suffixes to words ending l
> **4–9:** word meanings; prefixes: in, im
> **10:** shortened words; formal and informal vocabulary

Write the word to go with the definition.
Clue: starts with in or im

4 indefinite   not fixed, unclear
5 incomplete   unfinished
6 immature   childish
7 immobile   fixed, cannot be moved
8 improbable   not likely
9 inaccurate   wrong, not exact

10 Write the longer word to use in formal writing.

fridge refrigerator   **ref** referee
brill brilliant   **veg** vegetables

C Sentence work

Underline the main clause.

1 He waited for hours as the rain fell.

2 I enjoyed the game even though we lost.

Rewrite 1 and 2 above with the subordinate clause at the start.

3 As the rain fell, he waited for hours.

4 Even though we lost, I enjoyed the game.

Extend and improve the sentence. Include a relative clause.

5 A wizard sped down the street.
A wizard on a broomstick sped down the street, which was crowded with hovermobiles.

6 The little girl heard footsteps.
The little girl, who had lost her way in the woods, heard the patter of footsteps.

7 He saw a face.
He screamed when he saw the hideous face that appeared at the window.

Add a colon and continue the sentence with a list.

8 We divide the year up into four seasons: spring, summer, autumn and winter.

9 Abby checked her pockets: keys, pen, notebook and mobile phone.

10 For this trick you need a few simple objects: a hat, a rabbit and a magic wand.

> **PART C Focus**
> **1–4:** main and subordinate clauses; reordering clauses; use of commas
> **5–7:** using relative clauses
> **8–10:** use of a colon to introduce a list

X DEFINITIVE ANSWER   X SAMPLE ANSWER

A Warm-up

Read the headline. Then write the first sentence
of the article including a subordinate clause.

1 **United on cloud nine** Melton United fans
were ecstatic after their team had an
amazing 9-0 win over City.

2 **Thief caught red-handed** A thief was
arrested yesterday morning, while still
carrying the plant he had stolen.

Write two words related to the word in **bold**.

3 **apology** apologise, apologetic

4 **mystery** mysterious, mystify

5 **apply** application, reapply

6 **calculate** calculator, calculation

7 Make six verbs by adding prefixes to **act** and **do**.

undo, redo, overdo,
interact, react, overact

> **PART A Focus**
> **1–2:** subordinate clauses
> **3–6:** word families and related words
> **7:** verb prefixes
> **8–10:** spelling strategies

Add a short word to complete the longer word.

8 m e a sure m e n t   10 a c cord i n g l y

9 d i s a p point e d

B Word work

Add the suffixes to each root word to make three
new words.

ing ed ence

1 refer ring   refer red   refer ence

2 confer ring   confer red   confer ence

3 prefer ring   prefer ed   prefer ence

4 Underline the word that should have a hyphen.

reassure <u>reenter</u> reboot refill refuel

Add the correct prefix.

> **PART B Focus**
> **1–3:** adding suffixes to words ending **fer**
> **4:** prefixes with hyphens
> **5–7:** prefixes; word meanings
> **8–10:** words with subject-specific meanings

5 The footballer signed a new con tract.

6 I can dis tract him while you escape.

7 Nothing will de tract from her success.

Write a definition.

8 **pitch** (in music) tone, high or low

9 **pitch** (in sport) an area for playing on

10 **pitch** (in camping) to put up (a tent)

C Sentence work

Combine the three sentences into one. Do it in four different ways.

It was still snowing. Amy rushed outside. She made a snowman.

1 While it was still snowing, Amy rushed outside and made a snowman.

2 It was still snowing so Amy rushed outside and made a snowman.

3 Amy rushed outside while it was still snowing to make a snowman.

4 As Amy rushed outside to make a snowman, it was still snowing.

Write three alternatives for the word in **bold**. They do not have to be synonyms.

5 **The** people were shouting. Many, Two, Some

6 The dog was **on** the table. by, under, beside

7 Write the name of the class of words that you used

in Q5: determiners   **in Q6:** prepositions

Draw a line to the name of the punctuation mark used between the clauses.

8 That morning, I was very late; Ben had already left.   colon

9 We were delighted: the party had been a success.   comma

10 When I eventually arrived, it was too late.   semi-colon

> **PART C Focus**
> **1–4:** forming sentences with more than one clause
> **5–7:** word classes: determiners and prepositions
> **8–10:** identifying colons and semi-colons

X **DEFINITIVE ANSWER**   X **SAMPLE ANSWER**

A Warm-up

Reorder the words to make three different sentences.

was Jake sitting there beside her

1. There was Jake, sitting beside her.
2. There, sitting beside her, was Jake.
3. Sitting beside her, there was Jake.

Underline the possessive pronoun that is hidden in each word.

4. determi**ne**d   5. pro**fit**s

Underline the preposition that is hidden in each word.

6. ord**in**ary   7. rec**over**y

Write an adverb using the word in **bold**.

8. **probable**   probably

9. **possible**   possibly

10. Underline the verb to which you can add all these prefixes.

re im dis

claim cover <u>prove</u> press

PART A Focus
1–3: varying word order
4–7: word classes; visual spelling strategies
8–9: adverbs; **ably**, **ibly**
10: verb prefixes

B Word work

Add the missing syllables.

1. con / tro / ver / sy
   Clue: strong disagreement about an issue

2. ap / pre / hen / sive
   Clue: anxious

3. op / por / tu / ni / ty
   Clue: a chance to do something

4. il / lu / mi / nate
   Clue: light up

PART B Focus
1–4: spelling strategies for words that are often misspelt
5–7: root words; suffixes; word classes
8–10: using word structure to work out the meaning of technical words

Write a noun and an adjective related to the verb.

5. **create**   creation, creative

6. **vary**   variety, various

7. **imagine**   imagination, imaginary

Write a definition.
Clue: found in a book about the Moon

8. **weightlessness**   having no weight

9. **uninhabitable**   no-one can live there

10. **spherical**   round like a ball

C Sentence work

Add the missing punctuation.

1. Simon turned. It was the same voice. Yes, there was the mysterious stranger.

2. There was a crash. Stella jumped. She clutched the chair, waiting.

PART C Focus
1–2: punctuating main clauses; use of commas
3–4: subject and object
5–7: linking adverbials for cohesion
8–10: using language for effect; figurative language

Add a subject and an object to complete the sentence.

3. Alfie **dropped** the mobile phone.   4. Police **caught** the criminals.

Write three adverbials that could be used

5. **to show a result**   as a result, consequently, as a consequence

6. **to add more information**   also, furthermore, moreover

7. **to put a different view**   however, in contrast, on the other hand

Continue the sentence with a simile or a metaphor that creates a feeling of

8. **panic**   The crowd moved like a huge animal fleeing from danger.

9. **calm**   The wind was a gentle giant softly rustling the trees.

10. **excitement**   The acrobat flew through the air like an arrow speeding to its target.

X DEFINITIVE ANSWER   X SAMPLE ANSWER

A Warm-up

The Tardis has disappeared.

Write the next three sentences.

> PART A Focus
> 1–3: sentence types; structures
> 4–6: prefixes: ir, il, im
> 7–10: root words; word families

1 **an exclamation** What a disaster!

2 **a question** What has happened to the Doctor?

3 **a possibility** Maybe the Tardis has been captured by the Daleks and taken to their spaceship.

The ending of the word is missing. Write two suggestions as to what the complete word might be.

4 i l l u ___ illustrate, illuminate

5 i m m e ___ immense, immediate

6 i r r e ___ irregular, irrelevant

Write two words related to the word in **bold**.

7 **perform** performer, performance

8 **drama** dramatic, dramatically

9 **idea** ideal, idealist

10 **assist** assistant, assistance

B Word work

Add the same ending to all three words.

ery ary ory

1 diction ary   prim ary   ordin ary

2 gall ery   lott ery   cemet ery

3 categ ory   fact ory   direct ory

4 Make four words using these word parts only.

> PART B Focus
> 1–3: unstressed endings
> 4–8: roots and their meanings
> 9–10: antonyms and synonyms

graph auto bio y logy

autograph, biology, autobiography, biography

Write the meaning of the word part.

5 **auto** self

6 **graph** writing

7 **bio** life

8 **logy** the study of

9 Draw a line to match the antonyms.

dependable — unreliable
adequate — insufficient
required — unnecessary

10 Underline the two synonyms.

<u>havoc</u> haven harmony <u>disorder</u> distinct

C Sentence work

Add a subordinate clause that gives a contrasting idea. Use a different conjunction each time.

1 **Some believe that the fire was caused deliberately** while others say it was an accident.

2 **Hannah was trembling** as Kate stood over her, gloating.

3 **They continued to struggle** although their efforts were useless.

4 **City had the better first half,** whereas United were stronger in the second.

5 Underline the subject of this sentence. <u>Fire</u> destroyed acres of woodland.

6 Underline the object of this sentence. Fire fighters fought the <u>fire</u>.

7 Write a sentence using the word **flames** as the

> PART C Focus
> 1–4: adding subordinate clauses; using a range of conjunctions
> 5–7: subject and object
> 8–10: use of a colon, dash and brackets

subject Flames burnt the trees.

object Strong winds fanned the flames.

Continue the sentence after the punctuation mark.

8 **Many objects are made from wood:** tables, shelves, cupboards and pencils.

9 **The rock is very porous (** full of holes).

10 **The door slammed –** they were trapped!

A Warm-up

1 Write a two-clause sentence using these words.

book hair pencil

As she was reading the book, she idly
twisted her hair around the pencil.

Write two three-syllable words with the ending given.

2 **ture**   adventure   signature

3 **sure**   composure   exposure

4 **sion**   dimension   illusion

5 **tial**   initial   torrential

Write the suffix that makes all the words into verbs.

6 sharp tight bright deep light   en

7 idol equal final organ civil   ise

> **PART A Focus**
> **1:** forming two-clause sentences
> **2–5:** words ending **ture, sure, sion, tial**
> **6–7:** verb suffixes
> **8–10:** similes

Complete the simile.

8 **as springy as** elastic legs

9 **as welcome as** the start of spring

10 **as silent as** a falling snowflake

B Word work

Add the correct ending to the adjectives.

1 transpar _ent_

2 toler _ant_

3 eleg _ant_

4 conveni _ent_

> **PART B Focus**
> **1–4:** unstressed endings **ant, ent**
> **5–8:** rules for adding suffixes to words ending **fer** and **ge**
> **9–10:** formal and informal word choice

Write a noun related to the word in **bold**.

5 **confer**   conference

6 **infer**   inference

Write an adjective related to the word in **bold**.

7 **courage**   courageous

8 **recharge**   rechargeable

Write a more formal synonym for the word in **bold**.

9 It was **wrecked**.   destroyed

10 We **ditched** it.   discarded

C Sentence work

Is the sentence active or passive? Write your answer.

1 **The case was closed.**   passive

2 **A stranger opened the door.**   active

3 **Rain destroyed the crops.**   active

> **PART C Focus**
> **1–5:** active and passive voice
> **6–8:** varying sentences for effect; sentences with main and subordinate clauses
> **9–10:** punctuation: full stops, commas, inverted commas, apostrophes

Rewrite the active sentences as passive sentences.

4 The door was opened by a stranger.   5 The crops were destroyed by rain.

Continue the sentence so that it builds up suspense. Add a subordinate and a main clause.

6 **I followed the path** as it twisted through the sinister tangle of branches and it led me
into the heart of the forest.

Write two short contrasting sentences to follow the long one that you have just written.

7 A twig snapped close by.   8 What was it?

Punctuate the extract.

9 Charlie, now aged 92, remembers Ilford as it was. "There was Wilson's dairy," he recalls.

10 Julia Hopkins, who judged the competition, said, "Nikki's poster is really eye-catching."

X DEFINITIVE ANSWER   X SAMPLE ANSWER

A Warm-up

Write a pun based on the homophones.

1 **hair/hare** This dog caused a hare-raising experience.

2 **right/write** The book launch was all write on the night.

3 **sent/scent** This perfume is heaven scent.

4 **you/ewe** "It's all right for ewe," says cow to sheep outside burger bar.

Underline the words that do **not** have a plural form.

> **PART A Focus**
> **1–4:** puns
> **5:** unusual plurals
> **6–7:** word classes
> **8–10:** prefixes

5 child furniture goose advice

Use the word **charge** as a

6 **noun** There is a charge to go in.

7 **verb** I must charge my phone.

Add the same prefix to all three words.

8 de fault   de flate   de compose

9 co- owner   co- driver   co- star

10 en large   en grave   en trust

B Word work

Cross out the words that are wrongly spelt.
Write the correct spellings.

1 I made ~~freequent jurneys~~ to ~~foregn~~ lands.
frequent, journeys, foreign

2 I ~~past~~ many ~~familier~~ towns in the ~~reegon~~.
passed, familiar, region

3 I ~~reecrgnised~~ many ~~ansient structchers~~.
recognised, ancient, structures

Underline the root and write its meaning.

4 <u>popular</u> <u>population</u> <u>populate</u>
people

5 <u>pedal</u> <u>pedestrian</u> <u>pedometer</u>
foot

6 <u>aeroplane</u> <u>aerospace</u> <u>aerosol</u>
air

> **PART B Focus**
> **1–3:** common spelling errors
> **4–7:** meaning of roots
> **8–10:** synonyms for conjunctions

7 <u>prime</u> <u>primary</u> <u>primrose</u>
first

Write two synonyms to use in formal writing.

8 **plus**   additionally, moreover

9 **so**   consequently, therefore

10 **then again** on the contrary, alternatively

C Sentence work

Rewrite the sentence in the passive voice.

1 City won the game.   The game was won by City.

2 The mayor presented the prize.   The prize was presented by the mayor.

3 Jaguar made the car in 1961.   The car was made by Jaguar in 1961.

4 The waves splashed the spectators.   The spectators were splashed by the waves.

The old lady glared at the boy.

> **PART C Focus**
> **1–4:** changing active voice to passive
> **5–7:** varying sentence structure
> **8–10:** commas after fronted adverbials; using a dash between main clauses

Add more detail to this sentence by adding

5 **a relative clause** The old lady glared at the boy who was loitering suspiciously by the gate.

6 **a parenthesis** The old lady – clearly, not very happy – glared at the boy.

7 **another main clause** The old lady glared at the boy and he glared back.

Punctuate the sentence by adding a comma and a dash.

8 Although desperate to finish, he couldn't walk any further—the pain was too bad.

9 If you want the best, try Zoom trainers—they're great!

10 When he heard this, Joe began to laugh—he knew the truth at last.

Remind the pupil to complete Section 1 of the Progress chart on page 46 of the pupil book.

X **DEFINITIVE ANSWER**   X **SAMPLE ANSWER**

Writing task assessment sheet: The happening

Name: _____   Class/Set: _____

Teacher's name: _____   Date: _____

Sentence structure and punctuation

	Always/often	Sometimes	Never
Sentences are varied in length, using main and subordinate clauses including relative clauses			
Parenthesis is used for variety and economy			
Adverbials are used to add detail or to comment on events			
Expanded noun phrases are used to inform and describe			
A range of conjunctions and relative pronouns is used			
Use of tense is consistent with varied time references (e.g. progressive, perfect forms)			
Modal verbs and adverbs are used to suggest possibility			
Sentences are shaped for effect (e.g. fronting adverbials)			
Sentences are demarcated accurately			
Direct speech is set out and punctuated correctly			
Commas are used to mark phrases and clauses			
Apostrophes are used correctly			
Commas, brackets and dashes are used for parenthesis			
A single dash or colon is used correctly			

Composition and effect

Character, setting and events are developed to match chosen genre and to develop atmosphere			
Events are shaped into paragraphs to develop events			
Relationships between paragraphs are made clear (e.g. using adverbials, pronouns, repeated words)			
Story is developed through selection of detail, and actions are integrated with dialogue			
Features and techniques drawn from stories read are used, including use of figurative language			
Vocabulary is chosen for clarity and effect			

Spelling

Knowledge of spelling patterns is applied correctly			
Correct spelling of words that are often misspelt			
Homophones are correct			
Common roots, prefixes and suffixes are correct			
Rules for adding suffixes are applied and exceptions are correct			

Completed proofreading task: Flood alert

Name: _____ Class/Set: _____

Teacher's name: _____ Date: _____

All day, water levels have continyued to rise, threat^ening many homes.

Mr Jackson, the chief flood officer, said, "^Oof co^uarse, many people are feeling anxtious. ^aAnd we are offer_ring advi^cse and assistence wherever possⁱable."

The floods have also caused c^haos across the transport s^yistem. Earlier today, police called the roads 'tre^acher^ous' and said that people ^oaught to remain in their homes. ^Ssome drivers' cars were underwater.

Eric Brown, an ex₋police officer who lives in the village, told us he could not believe how quickly the water rose. He said, "^Wwe're just rel^{ie}eved to be safe."

Even though there has been torrensh^{ti}al rain for sev^ear^ael days, it seems people rec^{ei}ieved no offi^csial warning.

A^ccording to weather for^ecasters, more rain is expected this evening so the situation could possibl_ey worsen.

Section 1 tasks summary

A Warm-up

Rewrite the sentence. Use more interesting nouns and verbs and add an extra detail.

1. The woman gets out of the car.

   The film star emerges from her
   limousine to an explosion of flash bulbs.

2. The dog looked at the man.

   The bulldog peered at the postman with
   a look of hatred.

3. The man came into the room.

   The judge swept into court carrying a
   a pile of papers.

Add one letter to make a grammar term.

4. smile *simile*

5. cause *clause*

6. phase *phrase*

7. nun *noun*

> **PART A Focus**
> **1–3:** precise word choice for effect
> **4–7:** grammar terms
> **8–10:** root words; word classes

Write two nouns related to the word in **bold**.

8. **destroy** *destroyer, destruction*

9. **apply** *applicant, application*

10. **equal** *equality, equaliser*

B Word work

Add a prefix and/or suffix to complete the words.

1. script *ure*   pre script *ion*   manu script

2. verb *al*   ad verb *ial*   ad verb

3. part *icular*   im part *ial*   im part

Write the correct spelling of the underlined word.

4. much <u>resistence</u> *resistance*

5. a <u>dorment</u> volcano *dormant*

6. a strange <u>substence</u> *substance*

7. a good <u>influance</u> *influence*

> **PART B Focus**
> **1–3:** word structure; word families
> **4–7:** words ending **ence**, **ance**, **ant**
> **8–10:** words with subject-specific meanings

Write a definition of the word in **bold**.

8. the **seabed** *the bottom of the sea*

9. the cube's **volume** *the amount of space*
   in a 3D shape

10. a **litter** of three *a family of baby animals*

C Sentence work

Rewrite the information as a single sentence with a relative clause. Do it in two different ways.

Oxygen is a gas. It is found in the air. It is essential to life.

1. *Oxygen is a gas that is found in the air and is essential to life.*

2. *The gas oxygen, which is found in the air, is essential to life.*

3. Why do the single sentences sound better? *They are more concise.*

Rewrite the sentence, adding a preposition phrase to modify the subject of the sentence.

4. The cat chased the mouse. *The cat with one eye chased the mouse.*

5. The man saw the accident. *The man from the corner shop saw the accident.*

6. The birds ate the seeds. *The birds on the birdfeeder ate the seeds.*

One day almost five years later the man returned.

Punctuate the sentence using

> **PART C Focus**
> **1–3:** forming sentences with relative clauses
> **4–6:** noun modifiers: prepositions; subject of sentence
> **7–10:** commas, brackets and dashes to indicate a parenthesis

7. **commas** *One day, almost five years later, the man returned.*

8. **brackets** *One day (almost five years later) the man returned.*

9. **dashes** *One day – almost five years later – the man returned.*

10. What are the different effects of these punctuation marks? *Brackets and dashes cut off the*
    information more definitely. Commas cause less of a break in the sentence.

X **DEFINITIVE ANSWER**   X **SAMPLE ANSWER**

A Warm-up

Add three adverbs to make a sentence that says **when**, **how** and **where**.

1. _Yesterday_ it rained _heavily everywhere_ .

2. _Today_ we played _happily outdoors_ .

3. The man _always_ waits _patiently outside_ .

Make a word that ends and a word that starts with each letter string.

4. _ener_ **gy** → **gy** _mnastics_

5. _mer_ **cy** → **cy** _cle_

6. _geogra_ **phy** → **phy** _sical_

PART A Focus
1–3: use of adverbs
4–6: letter strings; spelling strategies
7–10: homophones

Write a sentence using the homophones.

7. **herd/heard** _The herd heard a sound._

8. **whale/wail** _The whale let out a wail._

9. **dear/deer** _"Oh dear," said the deer._

10. **steel/steal** _Who would steal a steel bin?_

B Word work

Write the adjective related to the noun.

1. **nutrition** _nutritious_

2. **suspicion** _suspicious_

Write the verb and noun related to the word in **bold**.

3. **insistent** _insist_ _insistence_

4. **defiant** _defy_ _defiance_

Add the missing syllables.

5. im / _me_ / _di_ / _ate_ / ly
Clue: straightaway

6. ap / _prox_ / _i_ / _mate_ / ly
Clue: roughly, about

7. ap / _pa_ / _rent_ / ly
Clue: seemingly

PART B Focus
1–4: using known words to spell other words: **tious/cious, ence/ance**
5–7: spelling strategies for tricky words
8–10: choosing synonyms

Write a synonym for the word in **bold**.

8. It was a **difficult** journey. _strenuous_

9. It is a **difficult** problem. _complex_

10. He can be **difficult**. _troublesome_

C Sentence work

Complete the sentence using these words. Circle the main clause in the sentence.

orange football

1. Although _the orange was large,_ (it was not as big as a football).

2. After _playing football for an hour,_ (they were glad of the orange juice).

3. As _it is the team's colour,_ (I wear an orange football scarf).

What a mess! You wouldn't believe it. Norma's cottage? More like Nor-mess cottage!

4. Underline the word that best describes the style of this text.   formal   traditional   <u>informal</u>

Give three reasons to explain your choice.

5. _The questions and exclamations make it sound like informal speech._

6. _Contractions are used in informal speech and writing._

7. _Short or incomplete sentences are informal._

PART C Focus
1–3: constructing sentences; clauses
4–7: structures and features of informal speech and writing
8–10: commas to avoid ambiguity

Add the comma or commas needed to make the meaning of the sentence clear.

8. Have you tried jogging before, Emma?

9. Giraffes, which have long necks, can reach food from tall trees.

10. According to Bharat, James is often late.

X DEFINITIVE ANSWER   X SAMPLE ANSWER

A Warm-up

Use the words **pigeon** and **wall** in a sentence using

(1) **a parenthesis** The pigeon, which landed on the wall, was enormous.

(2) **two main clauses** The pigeon was sitting on the wall but then it flew away.

(3) **a conjunction** I fell off the wall because I glimpsed an enormous pigeon.

Complete the mnemonic, which helps you to spell the word at the end of the sentence.

(4) You find a dent in an acci dent .

(5) There is a rat in sepa rat e.

(6) Put a pet in a com pet ition.

(7) Find out who met in a ce met ery.

Write two words related to the word in **bold**.

(8) **identity** identify, identical

(9) **belief** believe, disbelief

(10) **human** humane, humanity

PART A Focus
1–3: varying sentence structures
4–7: spelling strategies; mnemonics
8–10: root words

B Word work

Write the word to go with the definition.
The word begins with one of these prefixes.

il im ir

(1) improbable   unlikely

(2) illusion   a false idea

(3) irreversible   cannot be changed back or undone

PART B Focus
1–3: spelling words with prefixes; suffixes
4–6: i before e spelling rule; exceptions
7–10: formal vocabulary

Add **ei** or **ie** to make the long **ee** sound.

(4) d e c ei t   y ie l d   s ei z e

(5) r e l ie v e   s ie g e   p r o t ei n

(6) Which two words in questions 4 and 5 do **not** follow the normal 'i before e' rule?

'seize' and 'protein'

Write a more formal synonym for the word in **bold**.

(7) Leave your **stuff** here.   possessions

(8) It was **okay**.   acceptable

(9) They **put up** the price.   increased

(10) Knock before you **go in**.   enter

C Sentence work

Complete the sentence so that it follows this one.

Rays from the sun can be harmful.

(1) For example, they can damage your skin.

(2) Furthermore, looking at the sun directly can harm your eyes.

(3) As a result, it is important to use skin protection and wear sunglasses.

(4) However, don't let this spoil your summer fun.

Cross out the verb. Change it to the present perfect form.

(5) We ~~are holding~~ have held talks with the shop's owner.

(6) The plants ~~are beginning~~ have begun to grow.

(7) The wind ~~is doing~~ has done a lot of damage.

(8) Miss Hawkins ~~is teaching~~ has taught us about plants.

PART C Focus
1–4: linking adverbials; cohesive devices
5–8: verb tenses: the perfect form of verbs
9–10: use of semi-colons in lists; noun phrases

Add three more noun phrases to the list.

(9) The room was full of treasure: necklaces of glistening stones; rings with the reddest of rubies; diamonds like pieces of ice; bags of gold coins.

(10) He created a sumptuous feast: plates of roasted meats; steaming bowls of fresh vegetables; warm, oven-fresh pastries; rich, creamy cakes.

X DEFINITIVE ANSWER   X SAMPLE ANSWER

A Warm-up

Rewrite the sentence, changing the word order.

A figure appeared slowly, as the mist faded.

1. Slowly, as the mist faded, a figure appeared.

2. As the mist faded, a figure slowly appeared.

3. As the mist faded, a figure appeared slowly.

Write a word with the ending given.

4. **ion**   million

5. **cious**   delicious

6. **tious**   ambitious

PART A Focus
1–3: reordering sentences for effect
4–6: words ending ion, cious, tious
7–10: subject and object

Add a subject and an object.

7. The author   **wrote**   a book.

8. Mason   **packed**   the bags.

9. The dog   **caught**   the stick.

10. The elephant   **drank**   the water.

B Word work

Write sentences using the word **just** as an

1. **adverb**   It just happened.

2. **adjective**   It was a just verdict.

3. Add suffixes to make **just** into a

   verb   justify

   noun   justice

PART B Focus
1–2: homonyms; word classes
3: suffixes to change word class
4: word families
5–8: silent letters
9–10: common roots

4. Write three more words related to the word **just**.

   justly   justified   adjust

Add the silent letter.

5. k n i g h t   k n e a d   k n a v e

6. w r e a t h   w r e n c h   w r a t h

7. a u t u m n   h y m n   c o l u m n

8. l a m b   l i m b   n u m b

Write three words that end with the letters in **bold**.

9. **clude**   conclude, include, preclude

10. **gram**   anagram, diagram, pictogram

C Sentence work

Rewrite the sentence in the passive voice.

1. **A security man guarded the painting.** The painting was guarded by a security man.

2. **Dr Gill organised the competition.** The competition was organised by Dr Gill.

3. **The mud ruined her shoes.** Her shoes were ruined by the mud.

4. **The emperor saved the kingdom.** The kingdom was saved by the emperor.

5. **How is the passive version different?** It makes the receiver of the action the subject of the sentence.

Continue the sentence with a relative clause. Create a different mood in each sentence.

6. **He came to a room** which was lit by hundreds of tiny candles.

7. **He came to a room** where discarded newspapers lay on the bare wooden floor.

Punctuate the sentences. Use different punctuation marks in each one.

8. It seemed to me, or perhaps I imagined it, that the old man smiled.

9. If she fails—as I think she will—we must go on alone.

10. The planets orbit (travel round) the Sun.

PART C Focus
1–5: changing active voice to passive
6–7: creating contrasting moods; relative clauses
8–10: commas, brackets and dashes to indicate a parenthesis

X DEFINITIVE ANSWER   X SAMPLE ANSWER

SECTION 2 | Test 5

A Warm-up

Use the words **car** and **tree** in a sentence using

(1) **the active voice** The car hit a tree.

(2) **the passive voice** The tree was damaged by the car.

(3) **a conjunction** The car hit the tree as it suddenly turned left.

(4) **a relative clause** The car that I saw was parked under the tree.

Make a word that ends and a word that starts with each letter string.

PART A Focus
1–4: varying sentence type
5–7: letter strings; spelling strategies
8–10: spelling; linking adverbials

(5) lea **gue** → **gue** ss

(6) forei **gn** → **gn** aw

(7) uni **que** → **que** stion

Complete the spelling of the linking adverb.

(8) c o n s equently   **Clue:** as a result

(9) s u b s equently   **Clue:** afterwards

(10) i n i tially   **Clue:** at first

B Word work

(1) Add the correct prefix.

post pre

PART B Focus
1–3: prefixes and their meanings
4–8: spelling rules and exceptions
9–10: figures of speech

pre caution   post script   pre cede

Write the meaning of the prefix.

(2) **pre** before   (3) **post** after

Add **able** or **ible**.

(4) vis ible   detest able   resist ible

(5) formid able   accept able   aud ible

Which two words above do **not** follow the usual **able/ible** pattern?

(6) formidable   (7) resistible

(8) What is the normal rule for adding **able** and **ible**?

'able' is added to a complete recognisable word and 'ible' to a stem

Write a definition of the well-known saying.

(9) **in the limelight** the centre of attention

(10) **to be given the sack** to lose your job

C Sentence work

Ravi waited by the door.

PART C Focus
1–3: adding subordinate clauses
4–7: features of informal writing
8–10: use of a colon

Rewrite the sentence, adding a subordinate clause to the

(1) **beginning** When it was time to leave, Ravi waited by the door.

(2) **middle** Ravi, who had seen exactly what happened, waited by the door.

(3) **end** Ravi waited by the door until the others had gone.

Does the text sound formal or informal?

(4) Anita was born in 1948 in King's Norton, part of Birmingham.   formal

(5) Just in from college. What a day!   informal

Give two features used in the informal text that are not found in formal writing.

(6) an incomplete sentence   (7) an exclamation

Add a colon and complete the sentence.

(8) He couldn't read the letter: the handwriting was atrocious.

(9) She read the address on the note: it was 6 Park Street.

(10) Evie read the opening words: 'Once upon a time there was a daydreamer named Flo.'

22

A Warm-up

Continue the sentence after the conjunction.

1. The clown danced even though *he felt sad.*

2. The clown danced as if *he were a clockwork toy.*

3. The clown danced whenever *the music played.*

Add a suffix to make the word into a verb.

4. crystal *lise*

5. beauty *ify*

6. critic *ise*

7. identity *fy*

Put the letters in order to make a word.

8. **o g h u t** *tough*

9. **o g u h c** *cough*

10. **o g h t u f** *fought*

> **PART A Focus**
> **1–3:** using a range of conjunctions
> **4–7:** suffixes to form verbs
> **8–10:** words with letter string **ough**

B Word work

Add the ending to complete the adverb.

1. consider *ably* **Clue:** *very much*

2. notice *ably* **Clue:** *quite clearly*

3. incred *ibly* **Clue:** *amazingly*

Complete the word sum.

4. **curious** + ity = *curiosity*

5. **generous** + ity = *generosity*

6. **vapour** + ise = *vaporise*

7. **glamour** + ise = *glamorise*

8. Explain why these words do not follow usual spelling rules.

   Because you drop the 'u' in 'our' or 'ous' when adding the suffix.

> **PART B Focus**
> **1–3:** adverbs; words ending **ably**, **ibly**
> **4–8:** spelling rules; exceptions
> **9–10:** subject-specific meanings

Write a definition.

9. **metre** (in maths) *a unit for measuring length*

10. **metre** (in poetry) *rhythm*

C Sentence work

Rewrite the sentence with the adverbial at the beginning.

1. He stepped onto the stage despite his nerves. *Despite his nerves, he stepped onto the stage.*

2. The door opened as she stood there weeping. *As she stood there weeping, the door opened.*

3. What is the effect of reordering the sentences? *It draws attention to the characters' feelings.*

The door opened.

Rewrite the sentence as a multi-clause sentence with detail to match the story type.

> **PART C Focus**
> **1–3:** effects of reordering clauses
> **4–6:** composing multi-clause sentences
> **7–10:** use of punctuation

4. **school story** *The bell rang, the door opened and the class spilled out into the corridor.*

5. **mystery** *Slowly, the door opened and a figure moved silently into the room.*

6. **sci-fi** *As Blake placed his palm on the ID pad, the lab door opened automatically.*

Why are the punctuation marks needed in the sentence?

Phoebe is now my ex-best friend – I mean it this time.

7. **hyphen** *joins a prefix to a word*

8. **dash** *to link the two main clauses*

Em says it's my fault (but she would say that, wouldn't she?).

9. **comma** *to separate a question tag*

10. **apostrophes** *for contractions*

X DEFINITIVE ANSWER   X SAMPLE ANSWER

A Warm-up

Cross out the noun and complete the simile with an interesting and original noun phrase.

1. as white as ~~snow~~

   the first snowdrop of spring

2. as quiet as a ~~mouse~~

   butterfly's fluttering wings

3. as deep as the ~~sea~~

   ocean's unexplored depths

Write in full the word that the short form stands for.

4. **ID**   *identity*

5. **pro**   *professional*

6. **ad**   *advertisement*

7. **demo** *demonstration*

Write the missing letters.
Clue: small books

8. b r o *chure*

9. p a m *phlet*

10. c a t *alogue*

PART A Focus
1–3: similes; noun phrases
4–7: spelling; short forms of longer words
8–10: spelling patterns: ch, ph, gue

B Word work

Add the same ending to make three nouns.

1. accept *ance*   guide *ance*   ignore *ance*

2. insist *ence*   exis *tence*   occur *rence*

Change the ending on the adjective to write the related noun.

3. **frequent**   *frequency*

4. **vacant**   *vacancy*

PART B Focus
1–4: words ending ance, ence, ancy, ency
5: spelling strategies for words that are often misspelt
6: silent letters
7–10: figures of speech

5. Add a short word to complete the longer word.

   c o m *pan* y   e m *bar* r a s s

   e n v *iron* m e n t   v e *get* a b l e

6. Write the word correctly.

   thisle *thistle*   doutful *doubtful*

Add the same word to complete both figures of speech.

7. in *hot* pursuit; too *hot* to handle

8. the *heat* is on; in the *heat* of the moment

9. out *cold* ; make your blood run *cold*

10. a *cool* customer; keep your *cool*

C Sentence work

Complete the subordinate clause to add a condition.

PART C Focus
1–4: conditional sentences
5–7: summaries; subordinate clauses
8–10: use of a semi-colon

1. The sponsored walk will go ahead on Friday unless *it rains.*

2. People would not drop litter if *there were more litter bins.*

3. Martin will be able to come, provided that *he is over his cold.*

4. They will be here soon, so long as *the traffic is not too bad.*

Write a one-sentence summary of the story that includes a subordinate clause.

5. **Cinderella**   *A young girl goes from rags to riches when she meets Prince Charming.*

6. **Goldilocks**   *A girl causes chaos in the bears' house, before she runs off on their return.*

7. **Robin Hood**   *A brave Sherwood Forest youth, who robs from the rich and gives to the poor, escapes the sheriff's best efforts to capture him.*

Add a semi-colon.

8. There was no choice; we had to leave.

10. Don't interrupt; I haven't finished.

9. The house was empty; nothing stirred.

X **DEFINITIVE ANSWER**   X **SAMPLE ANSWER**

A Warm-up

Write a question-and-answer joke based on the homonym.

1. **trunk** Where does an elephant pack?

   In its trunk.

2. **wave** Is the sea friendly?

   Yes, it waves.

3. **watch** What sort of dog ticks?

   A watchdog.

Add the same short word to complete both longer words.

4. d e s **tin** a t i o n   e x **tin** g u i s h
5. l i s **ten** e d   g l i s **ten** e d
6. f o **reign**   s o v e **reign**
7. g r a **dual**   i n d i v i **dual**

Add the missing letters.
Clue: story types

PART A Focus
1–3: homonyms; word play
4–7: spelling strategies
8–10: spelling patterns

8. m **y** s t e r **y**
9. s c i e n c e   f i c t **i** o n
10. a d **v** e n t **u** r e

B Word work

Add a word to complete each compound word.
Clue: conjunctions

1. _____ **there** fore
2. **hence** forward
3. _____ **never** theless
4. _____ **more** over

PART B Focus
1–4: formal conjunctions
5–6: spelling strategies for words that are often misspelt
7: silent letters
8–10: older vocabulary

5. Underline the prefix in each word.

   <u>dis</u>solve <u>con</u>science <u>cor</u>respond <u>ac</u>company

6. How does this help to spell the word correctly?

   Because you can see the prefix and the root word.

7. Add the silent letter. **b p**

   d e **b** t   r e c e i **p** t

   p l u m **b** i n g   **p** s a l m

Write a modern phrase that means the same.

8. **set forth**   set out
9. **yonder**   over there
10. **go thither**   go to that place

C Sentence work

Rewrite the sentence in the passive voice without mentioning the person or people responsible.

1. Jasper slew the dragon.   The dragon was slain.
2. The people sent a message.   A message was sent.
3. A servant had broken the mirror.   The mirror had been broken.
4. The postman had delivered the letter.   The letter had been delivered.

Complete the table with words and phrases used in formal and informal letters.

	formal	informal
5	domestic residence	home
6	Dear Sir or Madam	Hi!
7	in duplicate	with a copy

PART C Focus
1–4: passive voice
5–7: formal and informal language
8–10: use of a colon

Why has the colon been used?

8. There are three events: the sprint, long jump and high jump.   To introduce a list.
9. He read the words on the sign: Harborough Hall.   To introduce a piece of information.
10. He knew he was late: it was past nine o'clock.   To show where the new main clause begins.

X **DEFINITIVE ANSWER**   X **SAMPLE ANSWER**

A Warm-up

Write the next three sentences.

Harry slipped and fell into the mud.

1 As a result, *he was covered in mud from head to toe.*

2 Unfortunately, *he did not have a change of clothes with him.*

3 However, *he was almost home so he could soon get changed.*

Underline the word that **cannot** be a verb.

4 book float ring <u>planet</u> bat

5 pop spot <u>safe</u> snap bubble

6 light lead <u>year</u> note ferry

Add the missing letters.

7 m <u>y</u> t h o l o g y

8 m <u>y</u> s t i f y

9 h <u>y</u> p n o t i s t

10 s <u>y</u> m m e t r i c a l

PART A Focus
1–3: linking adverbials
4–6: word classes; meanings
7–10: spelling patterns; y sound spelt i

B Word work

1 Add the correct prefix. **sub anti micro**

anti freeze   *anti* dote   *anti* biotic

micro chip   *micro* -organism

sub merge   *sub* zero   *sub* terranean

Write the meaning of the prefix.

2 **anti** *against*

3 **micro** *very small*

4 **sub** *under*

PART B Focus
1–4: prefixes; word meanings; prefixes with hyphens
5: spelling patterns
6: silent letters
7–10: choosing synonyms

5 Add the same two letters to all the words.

m a *ch* i n e r y   h e a d a *ch* e

a r *ch* i t e c t   p a r a *ch* u t e

6 Add the missing letter.

e x *h* i b i t i o n   v e *h* i c l e

s i l *h* o u e t t e

Write a synonym for the word in **bold**.

7 Tigers **follow** their prey.   *stalk*

8 Police **follow** criminals.   *pursue*

9 **Follow** the rules.   *obey*

10 I couldn't **follow** the story.   *understand*

C Sentence work

Rewrite the sentence, adding two commas. Explain how the commas change the meaning.

1 The puppies which were brown soon found new homes.

The puppies, which were brown, soon found new homes.

2 The sentence now means *all the puppies found new homes, not just the brown ones.*

3 The children who were excited waited outside.

The children, who were excited, waited outside.

4 The sentence now means *all the children waited outside and they were all excited.*

Complete the verb table to show the past, past progressive and past perfect forms of the verbs.

eat	ate	was eating	**had eaten**
go	went	**was going**	had gone
take	took	was taking	had taken
blow	blew	was blowing	had blown

PART C Focus
1–4: commas to avoid ambiguity
5–8: verb tenses: progressive and perfect forms
9–10: varying sentence length; composing and punctuating sentences

9 Complete the sentence using fewer than 10 words: **Falling** *to the ground, they lay still.*

10 Complete the sentence using more than 20 words: **As Ruby** *walked across the playing field, she was glad of the soft breeze that cooled her face and calmed her troubled thoughts.*

X DEFINITIVE ANSWER   X SAMPLE ANSWER

A Warm-up

Add another clause to develop the idea. Do this in four different ways.

Jo was holding the key.

1. Jo was holding the key that we hoped would open the box.
2. Jo was holding the key because she had just opened the door.
3. Jo was holding the key and Luke was carrying the box.
4. When I opened the door, I saw that Jo was holding the key.

Write two words that end with

5. **eous**   hideous, courteous
6. **ious**   previous, glorious

Write the antonym.

7. **future**   past
8. **prefix**   suffix
9. **antonym**   synonym
10. **formal**   informal

> **PART A Focus**
> **1–4:** multi-clause sentences to develop ideas
> **5–6:** spelling patterns: ious, eous
> **7–10:** technical vocabulary; antonyms

B Word work

Write the common root and its meaning.

1. **astronaut astronomer asterisk**
   'astro' means star
2. **monorail monocle monologue**
   'mono' means single or one

Write the noun formed by adding **ance**.

3. **appear** appearance   **endure** endurance
4. **hinder** hindrance   **enter** entrance
5. Why are the spellings of the words in question 4 different?
   Because you drop the 'e' from 'er' when adding the ending.
6. Add the ending that makes these words into nouns.
   correspond ence   **excel** lence

Write the meaning of the formal word.

7. **endorse**   support
8. **pursue**   chase
9. **cease**   stop
10. **commence**   start

> **PART B Focus**
> **1–2:** meaning of roots
> **3–6:** words ending ance, ence; spelling exceptions
> **7–10:** formal vocabulary

C Sentence work

Why has the writer used the passive voice?

1. The temperature was taken every hour. Because it doesn't matter who took it.
2. The poor man had been robbed. Because the robbed man is the most important person.
3. The cloak had been cut to ribbons. Because it creates a mystery; we don't know who did it.

Use personification to complete the sentence.

4. The sun stretched out her fingers and touched the Earth.
5. The sea played with the tiny boats, tossing them around.
6. The car groaned and spluttered, reluctant to be woken.
7. The river gurgled happily as it tumbled along.

Punctuate the sentence using commas and a single dash.

8. There, carved into the wood, was a number—the number 1004.
9. Flinging open the door, he ran—desperately, he ran.
10. It was an amazing sight—the spitting, hissing serpent, with its staring eyes and open jaws, was slithering across the ground.

> **PART C Focus**
> **1–3:** effect of using the passive voice
> **4–7:** personification
> **8–10:** use of commas; use of a dash between clauses

X DEFINITIVE ANSWER   X SAMPLE ANSWER

A Warm-up

Complete the sentence using a metaphor or personification.

① **Daisies** peep shyly from between the blades of grass.

② **An aeroplane** is a silver bird soaring into the sky.

③ **Spring** lit up the world with her sunny smile.

Complete the table.

	adjective	noun	verb
④	real	reality	realise
⑤	visual	vision	visualise
⑥	social	society	socialise

Add the missing letters.
Clue: sources of information

⑦ d i c t i o n a r y

⑧ b i b l i o g r a p h y

⑨ e n c y c l o p e d i a

⑩ t h e s a u r u s

PART A Focus
1–3: use of imagery
4–6: suffixes; word classes
7–10: spelling; technical vocabulary

B Word work

① Add the correct ending. **logy phobia athlon**

dec athlon   bio logy   tri athlon

hydro phobia   zoo logy   claustro phobia

Draw a line to join the root to its meaning.

② athlon — fear of

③ logy — contest

④ phobia — the study of

PART B Focus
1–4: meaning of word roots
5–6: words that are often misspelt
7–8: using root words to help spelling; silent letters
9–10: meaning of proverbs

Add the missing vowels.

⑤ b e n e f i c i a l   ⑥ s e c r e t a r y

Underline the root.

⑦ **signal signature signpost unsigned**

⑧ Write the words in which the **g** is silent.

signpost, unsigned

Explain the meaning of the proverb.

⑨ **Don't count your chickens before they are hatched.** Don't assume too soon that things will work out as you expect.

⑩ **A fool and his riches are soon parted.** If you are foolish you will lose your money quickly.

C Sentence work

Add a subordinate clause that gives a condition.

① **I could borrow the bike** if I promised not to take it on the road.

② **He would be safe** so long as no-one saw him.

③ **The team would score more goals** if they had a better striker.

④ **You too can be a star player** if you have lessons.

Write the past perfect form of the underlined verb.

⑤ **No rain <u>fell</u> for many weeks; the ground was parched.**   had fallen

⑥ **The crops <u>failed</u> and the people were starving.**   had failed

⑦ Explain why the past perfect form is used in these sentences.

It shows that the first event happened earlier and led to the second.

Cross out the conjunction and replace it with a semi-colon.

⑧ Spring is nearly here; ~~so~~ buds will soon appear on the trees.

⑨ They whispered quickly; ~~because~~ there was not much time.

⑩ The light went out; ~~therefore~~ she could see nothing.

PART C Focus
1–4: forming conditional sentences
5–7: past perfect verb form
8–10: using semi-colons**

X DEFINITIVE ANSWER   X SAMPLE ANSWER

A Warm-up

Make the statement into a question.

1. It's a lovely day today, *isn't it?*
2. You will try again, *won't you?*

Dad failed his driving test three times.

Write the next two sentences. Use a linking adverbial in each.

3. *In contrast, Mum passed first time.*
4. *As a result, Mum is always criticising Dad's driving.*

Underline the word that is **not** linked by meaning.

5. bicycle binoculars <u>biography</u> biceps
6. decade decimal December <u>declare</u>

Add the missing letters.
Clue: occupations

7. plu <u>m</u> <u>b</u> e r
8. opti <u>c</u> <u>i</u> a n
9. secre <u>t</u> <u>a</u> r y
10. mech <u>a</u> <u>n</u> i c

PART A Focus
1–2: question tags
3–4: cohesion; linking adverbials
5–6: word roots; meanings
7–10: spelling patterns

B Word work

Add the missing letters.

1. envir <u>on</u> ment
2. gov <u>ern</u> ment
3. parl <u>ia</u> ment
4. soc <u>ie</u> ty

5. Add the correct word ending.

   ency ancy

   emerg <u>ency</u>   hesit <u>ancy</u>   frequ <u>ency</u>

PART B Focus
1–4: words that are often misspelt
5: words ending ency, ancy
6–8: root words; prefixes and suffixes
9–10: older vocabulary

Write two words formed from the root word.

6. **music** *musical, musician*
7. **moist** *moisten, moisture*
8. **mobile** *automobile, mobility*

Write a modern word or phrase that means the same.

9. **pauper** *beggar*
10. **wireless** *radio*

C Sentence work

Complete the sentence.

1. Limping *painfully, she struggled home.*
2. Frightened *by the sudden noise, the frogs dived into the water.*
3. Leaping *bravely, they crossed the stream.*
4. Holding *the candle high, they could just make out the ceiling.*

We like skateboarding so I guess a skateboard park would be great.

PART C Focus
1–4: constructing and punctuating sentences
5–7: formal and informal writing
8–10: dashes, colons and semi-colons between clauses

5. Underline the words that make this sentence sound personal and informal.
6. Rewrite the sentence to make it sound impersonal and formal.

   Many youngsters enjoy skateboarding so a skateboard park would be a useful facility.

7. When might you use the formal version? *in a formal piece of writing, for a public audience*

Punctuate the sentence.

8. Suddenly, there was a loud scream; everyone leapt to their feet.
9. A word of warning: don't try this at home!
10. At that moment, we realised there was no going back—it was too late!

Remind the pupil to complete Section 2 of the Progress chart on page 46 of the pupil book.

X DEFINITIVE ANSWER   X SAMPLE ANSWER

29

Writing task assessment sheet: Moving day

Name: _____ Class/Set: _____

Teacher's name: _____ Date: _____

Sentence structure and punctuation

	Always/often	Sometimes	Never
Sentences are varied in length, using main and subordinate clauses including relative clauses			
A variety of sentence types is used (e.g. questions/exclamations for an informal tone)			
A range of conjunctions and relative pronouns is used			
Use of tense is appropriate, including the perfect form			
Sentences are shaped for effect (e.g. fronting adverbials)			
Passive voice is used to maintain or change focus			
Expanded noun phrases are used to convey information concisely			
Sentences are demarcated accurately			
Inverted commas are used for direct quotes			
Commas are used to clarify meaning and avoid ambiguity			
Apostrophes are used correctly			
Commas, brackets and dashes are used for parenthesis			
A colon, semi-colon or dash is used between clauses			

Composition and effect

Features of diary form are used (e.g. personal comment, description of feelings)			
Grammar choices are appropriate to informal diary tone (e.g. questions, contractions, direct address)			
Paragraphs are used to develop events, ideas and themes			
Paragraphs and ideas are linked (e.g. using adverbials, pronouns, repeated words)			
Contrasting viewpoint is established and maintained (e.g. using comment, dialogue, detail)			
Vocabulary choices add to impact and informal style			

Spelling

Knowledge of spelling patterns is applied correctly			
Correct spelling of words that are often misspelt			
Homophones are correct			
Words with silent letters are correct			
Common roots, prefixes and suffixes are correct			
Rules for adding suffixes are applied and exceptions are correct			

Completed proofreading task: The rainforest

Name: _____ Class/Set: _____

Teacher's name: _____ Date: _____

Factual description

The rainforest is a very spe*c*sial envira*on*ment—a pre*ci*shous natural habitat that is home to a var*ie*eity of truely remark*a*ble plant's and animals.

Wherever light reaches the forest floor, e*c*xotic ferns fl*o*urish. While high above, the trees' branches form a can*n*opy of leaves and flowers, which is home to millions of cur*o*ius insects and animals. The trees provide these incredab*i*le creatures with a*n* essen*ti*shal supply of food: fruits, nuts, seeds and pol*l*en.

Poetic description

Trees of dizzying h*ei*ieght tangle together, forming a secret garden not vis*i*able from below. *A*amongst eleg*a*ent colum*n*s of greenery, brightly coloured flowers *e*intwine branches with their mouth's open to the insist*e*ant rain.

Only tiny chinks of light and the drip of rain can p*ie*eirce the darkness of the forest c*ei*ieling. Here, roots hang like ropes from anc*ie*eint bells.

Section 2 tasks summary

[blank box]

A Warm-up

Complete the subordinate clause.

1. **Jemma is happy as long as** she has her music to listen to.

2. **Jemma is happy until** she has to tidy her room.

3. **Jemma is happy while** Lucy is away on holiday.

4. **Jemma is happy although** she is sometimes homesick.

Add the missing letters.

5. **c h a m** eleo **n**
6. **c h a m** pagn **e**
7. **c h a m** pio **n**
8. **c h a n** delie **r**

PART A Focus
1–4: subordinate clauses; using a range of conjunctions
5–8: spelling patterns
9–10: word derivation

Explain the derivation.

9. **hyperlink** comes from the prefix 'hyper' (meaning beyond normal) and root word 'link' (meaning connection)

10. **cyber café** comes from the prefix 'cyber' and the word for a coffee house

B Word work

Write the correct spelling.

1. **comunication** communication
2. **prononsiation** pronunciation
3. **exagaration** exaggeration

Write two words that start with the prefix.

4. **mal** malfunction, malice
5. **multi** multiple, multitude

6. Write the meaning of the prefix.

mal bad, badly

multi many

PART B Focus
1–3: tricky words; common errors
4–6: meaning of prefixes
7–10: word meanings in different contexts

Write different definitions of each noun.

7. **rap** a sharp tap
8. **rap** a type of music
9. **cricket** an insect like a grasshopper
10. **cricket** a game played with bat and ball

C Sentence work

Rewrite the sentence so that the information given in brackets is included as a parenthesis.

1. **The gerbil is best suited to life in the desert. (UK – popular pet)** The gerbil, a popular pet in the UK, is best suited to life in the desert.

2. **Birds of prey include hawks and owls. (hawks hunt – day; owls hunt – night)** Birds of prey include hawks, which hunt during the day, and owls, which hunt at night.

3. **Edward Jenner pioneered vaccination. (b. 1749; a doctor)** Edward Jenner (a doctor born in 1749) pioneered vaccination.

Write the formal sentence so that it sounds informal.

4. **I am completely blameless.** I didn't do it.

5. **Refrain from conversing.** Stop chatting.

Write the informal sentence so that it sounds formal.

6. **You shouldn't do things like that.** Such behaviour is totally unacceptable.

7. **Sorry I can't help you.** Unfortunately, I am not able to assist you.

Write a sentence with direct speech to open the traditional story.

8. **Red Riding Hood** "Don't take that short cut," warned Red's mother.

9. **Snow White** "I love apples," said Snow White, taking a bite.

10. **Aladdin** "Put down that lamp and hurry up," came an impatient voice.

PART C Focus
1–3: relative clauses in a parenthesis using commas, brackets and dashes
4–7: using vocabulary and structures of formal writing
8–10: punctuating direct speech

X DEFINITIVE ANSWER   X SAMPLE ANSWER

A Warm-up

Write a sentence using the word **spell** as a

1 **verb** I can spell the word 'abracadabra'.

2 **noun** The wizard cast a spell and turned Jim into a frog.

Write a sentence using the word **caterpillars** as the

3 **subject** Caterpillars ate my plants.

4 **object** The boy observed the caterpillars.

Add the missing letters.

5 a p p r e ci a t e
6 f e r o ciou s
7 a r t i f i cia l
8 e f f i cie n t

> **PART A Focus**
> **1–2:** word classes
> **3–4:** subject and object
> **5–8:** spelling patterns
> **9–10:** word structure

Make three words.

9 **auto tele cue gram graph**
telegram, autograph, autocue

10 **med graph para ic al**
paramedic, medical, paragraph

B Word work

Complete the word to go with the definition.
Use a dictionary to check the spelling.

1 a n t icipate — expect to happen

2 a n t hology — collection of poems or stories

3 a n t agonism — dislike; hostility

4 a n t enna — aerial; one of the feelers on an insect

5 These words and prefixes are mixed up. Write them correctly.

webport **heli**lung **aqua**cam

heliport, webcam, aqualung

Write a more formal synonym.

6 **try** endeavour

7 **watch over** supervise

8 **ask for** request

9 **turn down** decline

10 **go ahead** proceed

> **PART B Focus**
> **1–4:** using a dictionary
> **5:** prefixes
> **6–10:** formal and informal word choice

C Sentence work

Complete the sentence.

1 **Hiding** her face behind a book, she crossed the room unnoticed.

2 **Balanced** precariously, he rescued the hat from the tree.

3 **Peering** over the banister, he could see the two figures arguing.

4 **Surprised** by the sudden attack, Dylan was unable to escape.

Edit the sentence. Cross out any repeated or unnecessary words.

5 He tried parachuting because he had always wanted to ~~try parachuting~~.

6 Mix the yeast into the flour and then add water ~~to the flour~~.

7 The ship was pounded by enormous waves and finally ~~the ship~~ sank.

> **PART C Focus**
> **1–4:** varying sentence construction
> **5–7:** use of ellipsis
> **8–10:** use of brackets to add a parenthesis

Use brackets to add a parenthesis giving extra explanation or examples.

8 Icebergs are formed when glaciers (rivers of ice) meet the sea.

9 Bread, pasta (such as spaghetti and macaroni) and some cereals are made from wheat.

10 Different types of figurative language (such as similes and metaphors) are used to create a mood or feeling.

X **DEFINITIVE ANSWER**   X **SAMPLE ANSWER**

A Warm-up

Write an advert for **Sam's soups** using features of informal writing.

1 **a contraction** You'll love Sam's soups.

2 **an exclamation** What a 'soup-er' idea!

3 **a question tag** You need something warm and tasty for lunch, don't you?

4 **informal words** Have a glug from a mug.

Add the missing letters.
Clue: types of boat

5 y a c h t

6 d i n g h y

7 c a n o e

PART A Focus
1–4: features of informal speech and writing
5–7: tricky spellings
8–10: prefixes; word structure

Write the prefix that can be added to all three words.

8 final colon circle semi

9 natural structure human super

10 hang power load over

B Word work

Add the same ending to all three words.

ary ery ory

1 direct ory   categ ory   dormit ory

2 rot ary   volunt ary   tribut ary

3 scen ery   jewell ery   machin ery

4 Complete the word to go with the definition.

ball ad   a song or poem

ball et   a type of dance

ball ot   a vote

PART B Focus
1–3: unstressed endings
4–6: word meanings and derivations; using a dictionary
7: word roots
8–10: homophones and words that are often confused

Read the words you made in question 4. Write the words that are derived from each meaning of the word **ball**. Use a dictionary to help you.

5 **ball** a dance   ballad, ballet

6 **ball** a round object   ballot

7 Write three words starting with the root **aero**.

aerobics, aerosol, aerodynamic

Cross out the incorrect words in the phrase.

8 a weather ~~vein~~ vane ~~vain~~

9 a ~~stationary~~ stationery shop

10 a steep **descent** ~~dissent decent~~

C Sentence work

Rewrite the sentence in the active voice to focus on the main character.

1 A sudden scream startled him.   He was startled by a sudden scream.

2 The swirling lights dazzled her.   She was dazzled by the swirling lights.

3 The man's strange clothing puzzled me.   I was puzzled by the man's strange clothing.

4 The sound of the sea calmed Ellie's mind.   Ellie's mind was calmed by the sound of the sea.

Improve the sentence. Add one or two adverbs for emphasis.

5 This is   absolutely   vital.

6 This creature is now   extremely   rare.

7 Safety   , most importantly,   is a big concern.

PART C Focus
1–4: use of the active and passive voice
5–7: editing: adding adverbs for emphasis; commas
8–10: use of a colon

Add a colon and complete the sentence.

8 There are five vowels: 'a', 'e', 'i', 'o' and 'u'.

9 These are examples of conjunctions: when, although, until.

10 The room was now completely empty: everyone had gone home.

X **DEFINITIVE ANSWER**   X **SAMPLE ANSWER**

A Warm-up

Complete the sentence with a relative clause.

1 There is a faraway kingdom where no-one ever smiles.

2 We went to a party where everyone dressed up as superheroes.

3 I remember the day when I started school.

Change one letter to make a homophone.

4 course — coarse

5 current — currant

6 dual — duel

PART A Focus
1–3: relative clauses using **where, when**
4–6: homophones
7: figures of speech
8–10: synonyms; using a thesaurus

7 Write in the missing animal.

That's put the cat among the pigeons.

Write a synonym for the word in **bold**. You can use a thesaurus.

8 The ground is **soggy**. saturated

9 I like **soft** colours. muted

10 It is a **stupid** idea. foolish

B Word work

Write the correct spelling of the animal group. You can use a dictionary.

1 verterbrate — vertebrate

2 amphibion — amphibian

3 mammel — mammal

PART B Focus
1–3: using a dictionary to check spellings
4–6: suffixes to change word class
7–10: words with more than one meaning; word classes

Use a suffix to make the noun into an adjective.

4 **triangle** — triangular

5 **geometry** — geometrical

6 **cylinder** — cylindrical

Write different definitions of each word.

7 **grate** (noun) part of a fireplace

8 **grate** (verb) shave into small bits

9 **hide** (noun) the skin of an animal

10 **hide** (verb) keep out of sight

C Sentence work

Reorder the sentence so that it starts with the adverbial and focuses on the feelings of the character.

1 He walked on although he was scared. Although he was scared, he walked on.

2 They followed the others, as if in a trance. As if in a trance, they followed the others.

3 Ed crawled into the cave despite the pain. Despite the pain, Ed crawled into the cave.

4 He stood up with a tingle of excitement. With a tingle of excitement, he stood up.

PART C Focus
1–4: reordering sentences for effect
5–7: cohesive devices
8–10: hyphens to avoid ambiguity

5 Write three phrases that introduce one side of an argument.

supporters argue, it is claimed that, some people believe that

6 Write three phrases that introduce a different opinion.

opponents point out, critics of this view argue that, those against argue

7 Write three adverbials that introduce an opposing view.

however, on the other hand, in contrast

Tick the sentence using a hyphen correctly.

8 Draw twenty-two dimensional shapes. | Draw twenty two-dimensional shapes. ✓

9 The deckchair was red-hot from the sun. ✓ | The deck-chair was red hot from the sun.

10 She is a well known film-star. | She is a well-known film star. ✓

A Warm-up

Use the words **goat** and **socks** in a sentence using the

1 **active voice** The goat ate my socks.

2 **passive voice** My socks were eaten by the goat.

3 **perfect tense** The goat has eaten my socks.

PART A Focus
1–3: varying sentence type and form
4–7: spelling strategies
8–10: homophones

Add the ending of the adjective.

4 **torren** tial   6 **substan** tial

5 **atro** cious   7 **cons** cious

Write a headline using a pun based on the homophones.

8 **main/mane** Safari park ready for mane event

9 **not/knot** String is knot a problem for scouts

10 **aloud/allowed** No girls aloud – girl band concert cancelled

B Word work

Add the same ending to all three words. **cial tial**

1 **essen** tial   **poten** tial   **influen** tial

2 **benefi** cial   **artifi** cial   **finan** cial

PART B Focus
1–2: words ending tial, cial
3–4: silent letters
5–6: prefixes
7–10: formal and informal word choice

Add the silent letter.

b g h n s t

3 s o l e m n   i s l e   c a m p a i g n

4 h u s t l e   e x h i b i t   s u b t l e

Add a different prefix to complete each of these space terms.

5 uni **verse**   super **nova**   tele **scope**

6 cosmo **naut**   atmo **sphere**   aster **oid**

Write a more formal synonym to replace the word or phrase in **bold**.

7 Be **on your guard**.   vigilant

8 It was **okay**.   satisfactory

9 The amount was **not enough**.   inadequate

10 The place was **unfriendly**.   inhospitable

C Sentence work

Shorten the sentence by starting with the verb, rather than a conjunction.

1 Although I was trembling with fear, I turned the key. Trembling with fear, I turned the key.

2 Because she was running fast, she quickly caught up. Running fast, she quickly caught up.

3 As he gathered his strength, he climbed higher. Gathering his strength, he climbed higher.

4 As I was encouraged by the applause, my confidence returned.
Encouraged by the applause, my confidence returned.

5 Underline the adjectives.   **Each snowflake is individual and unique.**

6 What do the adjectives tell us about the design of snowflakes? They are all different.

7 Underline the verbs.   **As the bulldozers advance, all wildlife flees.**

8 Why has the writer chosen these verbs? To make it sound as if the wildlife is under attack.

PART C Focus
1–4: editing: sentence variation
5–8: choosing words for meaning and effect
9–10: punctuating to clarify meaning; commas and hyphens to avoid ambiguity

9 Why is the comma needed in this sentence?   **Has the cat eaten, Jess?**
Without the comma, it sounds like the cat has eaten Jess.

10 Why is a hyphen needed in this sentence?   **I re-sent the emails.**
Without the hyphen, it sounds like the writer is upset or angry about the emails.

 X DEFINITIVE ANSWER   X SAMPLE ANSWER

A Warm-up

Change the preposition phrase. Write three different sentences.

The giant stomped over the hill

1. The giant stomped into the sea.
2. The giant stomped across the hillside.
3. The giant stomped through the forest.

Change the prefix to make a new word.

4. interrupt → erupt
5. transfer → defer
6. interaction → reaction
7. telescope → microscope

Underline the word that is wrongly spelt.

8. arguable adorable <u>agreable</u>
9. <u>dissbelief</u> disservice dissatisfy
10. referee <u>referal</u> reference

PART A Focus
1–3: preposition phrases
4–7: prefixes
8–10: spelling rules

B Word work

Write the correct spelling of the library sign.

1. gimnastiks and phisical edurcation
   gymnastics and physical education
2. moden forern langwages
   modern foreign languages
3. enginering, desine and tecknolergy
   engineering, design and technology

Write two words related to the word in **bold**.

4. **public**   publicity, publication
5. **memory**   memorable, memorial
6. **origin**   original, originate

Add the correct word.

larva lava

7. volcanic   lava
8. caterpillar   larva

symbols cymbals

9. I play the   cymbals.
10. There were   symbols   on the map.

PART B Focus
1–3: correcting spellings
4–6: word families and related words
7–10: homophones

C Sentence work

Rewrite the sentence in the passive voice to make it sound impersonal.

1. I sent a letter to the newspaper.   A letter was sent to the newspaper.
2. We will have to cancel the concert.   The concert will have to be cancelled.
3. We provide a choice of activities.   A choice of activities is provided.
4. I have taken steps to prevent this.   Steps have been taken to prevent this.

Write a question to follow the sentence. Form your questions in different ways.

5. Hanif ran towards the river.   Would he get there in time?
6. The path divided.   Which way now?
7. I left him to it.   Well, there was nothing I could do, was there?

PART C Focus
1–4: the passive voice in impersonal writing
5–7: forming questions; question tags
8–10: colons and semi-colons in lists

Insert a colon and a semi-colon in the correct place in the sentence.

8. We sell a range of snacks: rolls, which are homemade; cakes and delicious ice creams.
9. Strong gales can cause serious problems: roof tiles are dislodged; chimneys damaged and branches blown off trees.
10. How else could you present the information?   as a list with bullet points

A Warm-up

Continue the sentence using

1. **the active voice** The sword _pierced the knight's armour._

2. **the passive voice** The sword _had been found in the lake._

3. **a relative pronoun** The sword _that he held glinted in the sunlight._

Add a short word to complete the longer word.

4. g _has_ t l y
5. o _bed_ i e n t
6. a _band_ o n e d
7. j e _well_ e r y

> **PART A Focus**
> **1–3:** varying sentence type and form
> **4–7:** spelling strategies
> **8–10:** exploring word roots

Complete the sentence.

8. **Archaeology** is the study of _ancient remains._

9. **Etymology** is the study of _words._

10. Underline the **ology** that is **not** a real word.

    zoology meteorology <u>snowology</u> sociology

B Word work

Add the missing syllables.

1. ex / _tin_ / guish   **Clue:** _put out_
2. con / _so_ / nant   **Clue:** _not a vowel_

Add the prefix **pre** to complete the words.

3. _pre_ judice   _pre_ cede

4. Write the words by their meaning.

   precede   go before

   prejudice   a preconceived opinion

Write two words related to the word in **bold**.

5. **refer**   _reference, referee_
6. **govern**   _government, governor_

Cross out the incorrect word in the sentence.

7. Take my **advice** ~~advise~~.
8. ~~Practice~~ **Practise** every day.
9. Let's ~~device~~ **devise** a plan.

> **PART B Focus**
> **1–2:** spelling strategies; use of syllables
> **3–4:** using word structure
> **5–6:** using root words to help spelling
> **7–10:** homophones and words that are often confused

10. Complete these sentences about the words above.

    The verbs end _with 'ise'._

    The nouns end _with 'ice'._

C Sentence work

Complete the sentences to show two possible and two certain outcomes.

1. **If Jack had not climbed the beanstalk**, _he would not have become rich._
2. **If Cinderella had not lost her shoe**, _the prince would never have found her._
3. **If Goldilocks had not run away**, _the bears might have forgiven her._
4. **If the boy had not cried 'Wolf!'**, _then people might have believed him._

Rewrite the sentence using a more formal style.

5. **We shouldn't wear jeans to school.** _It is inappropriate to wear casual dress at school._
6. **The centre helps old people.** _The centre provides a valuable service for the elderly._
7. **People want the councillors to rethink.** _There is pressure on the council to reconsider._
8. **We want money to make up for the mess.** _We are seeking compensation for the damage._

9. Punctuate the information as **two** sentences, adding the capital letter where necessary.

   On average, a person in the UK uses 150 litres of water a day. In parts of Africa, each person has just ten litres a day.

> **PART C Focus**
> **1–4:** conditional sentences for supposition; modal verbs to show possibility
> **5–8:** using formal language and grammar
> **9–10:** using full stops or semi-colons between independent clauses

10. Punctuate it again as **one** sentence.

    On average, a person in the UK uses 150 litres of water a day; in parts of Africa, each person has just ten litres a day.

X **DEFINITIVE ANSWER**   X **SAMPLE ANSWER**

A Warm-up

The subject is **umbrellas**. Write a sentence using the given determiner.

1 **all** All umbrellas need to be waterproof.

2 **some** Some umbrellas are black while others are brightly coloured.

3 **these** These bright umbrellas look like a field of colourful mushrooms.

Add one letter to make a different word.

4 scare   scarce
5 through   thorough
6 lightning lightening

PART A Focus
1–3: determiners
4–6: spelling strategies
7–10: word origins

Draw a line to join the word to its language of origin.

7 patio ———— Norwegian
8 ski ———— Latin
9 chauffeur ———— Spanish
10 science ———— French

B Word work

Complete the word sum. Check the spelling carefully.

1 **humour + ous** = humorous

2 **disaster + ous** = disastrous

3 **miracle + ous** = miraculous

PART B Focus
1–3: spelling rules; exceptions
4–7: using a dictionary to check meaning
8–10: formal vocabulary

Use a dictionary to write the meaning of the word in **bold**.

4 a **lucid** account   clear, easy to follow
5 a **ludicrous** idea   stupid, absurd
6 a **melancholy** song   sad
7 a **mediocre** effort   not very good

Complete the unfinished words in these formal sentences.

8 All empl oyees   will be issued with a work per mit   .

9 Please en sure   that you pro vide   a contact number for use in an em ergency   .

10 Further details ava ilable   on re quest   .

C Sentence work

Rearrange the sentence so that the noun phrase comes at the end.

1 There was a huge bull right in front of me. There, right in front of me, was a huge bull.

2 There was the dog, staggering towards him, thin as a rake.
There, staggering towards him, thin as a rake, was the dog.

3 The giant beast slowly loomed out of a thin swirling mist.
Slowly, out of a thin swirling mist, loomed the giant beast.

He won the Olympics and then ~~he won~~ **the World Championships.**

4 Why has the writer crossed out the words? It makes sense without them.

5 What is this called? Tick one.   ambiguity   ellipsis ✓   subjunctive

PART C Focus
1–3: reordering sentences
4–5: using ellipsis
6–7: choosing words for effect
8–10: use of a dash, colon and semi-colon

Complete the sentence to create a sense of

6 **calm**   Sunlight rippled gently across the clear blue water.

7 **tension**   Darkness silently crept around them, closing in on its prey.

Continue the sentence using a dash, colon or semi-colon, and add another clause.

8 **This is a warning**: dogs can bite.

9 He waved his fist; we smiled back.

10 Now he was frightened — he was more frightened than ever before.

A Warm-up

A tiger has escaped from the local zoo.

Continue the sentence with

1. **an adverb** A tiger has escaped from the local zoo today.

2. **a semi-colon** A tiger has escaped from the local zoo; people are warned to be on alert.

3. **a conjunction** A tiger has escaped from the local zoo when his enclosure was left open accidentally.

Write the correct spelling.

4. receit — receipt

5. decietful — deceitful

6. concieve — conceive

> **PART A Focus**
> **1–3:** varying sentence structure
> **4–6:** ei spellings
> **7–10:** word derivations

Write the day of the week that means

7. day of the Moon — Monday

8. day of Saturn — Saturday

9. day of the god Woden — Wednesday

10. day of the god Thor — Thursday

B Word work

Write the correct spelling.

1. Law and justise in Anglo saxon comunties
   Law and justice in Anglo-Saxon communities

2. Roman arcitecture and militery strenth
   Roman architecture and military strength

3. Bronze age religon and cullture
   Bronze Age religion and culture

Write two words that start with the root.

4. **cert** certain, certificate

5. **spect** spectator, spectacle

6. **quad** quadrilateral, quadruple

> **PART B Focus**
> **1–3:** proofreading; checking spelling and punctuation
> **4–6:** roots; linked words
> **7–10:** word meanings in different contexts

Write different definitions of each word.

7. **mould (in arts and crafts)** to form a shape from a material

8. **mould (in science)** a kind of fungus

9. **scale (in science)** a small piece of skin on a snake or fish

10. **scale (in geography)** how distance is represented on a map

C Sentence work

Rewrite the sentence in the passive voice, without mentioning who is responsible.

> **PART C Focus**
> **1–3:** use of the passive voice to change focus
> **4–7:** expanded noun phrases
> **8–10:** use of a semi-colon between independent clauses

1. Man's actions force some animals to find new habitats.
   Some animals are forced to find new habitats.

2. Man hunted the dodo until it became extinct. The dodo was hunted to extinction.

3. People are cutting down large areas of forest. Large areas of forest are being cut down.

An apatosaurus was a huge plant-eating dinosaur with an enormously long neck.

4. Why does the writer use this expanded noun phrase? It gives a lot of information concisely.

Write your own expanded noun phrases.

5. The hippopotamus is a huge African animal with a barrel-shaped body.

6. A stegosaurus was a plant-eating dinosaur with a row of bony plates on its back.

7. A peacock is a male bird with a spectacular tail of brightly coloured feathers.

Put a tick if the sentence is correctly punctuated. Put a cross if it is not.

8. If commuters used public transport, the roads would be less crowded. ✓

9. Climate change is a huge concern, experts are worried about Earth's future. ✗

10. Write the incorrect sentence correctly.
    Climate change is a huge concern; experts are worried about Earth's future.

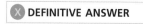 X DEFINITIVE ANSWER   X SAMPLE ANSWER

A Warm-up

Write a list of activities as bullet points.

1 There will be lots of fun activities:
   · a bouncy castle
   · a water slide
   · outdoor karaoke

2 Write a sentence that lists the same information.
   There will be lots of fun activities:
   a bouncy castle, a water slide and
   outdoor karaoke.

Write a word starting with these letters. You can use a dictionary to help you.

3 h y d rogen

4 h y g iene

5 h y p notist

6 h y s terical

> **PART A Focus**
> **1:** punctuating bullet points to list information
> **2:** colons and commas in lists
> **3–6:** using a dictionary
> **7–10:** word play

Use word play to write a name for a

7 **hairdresser** Headlines

8 **fish and chip shop** The Jolly Fryer

9 **flower shop** Busy Lizzy's

10 **bakery** The Upper Crust

B Word work

Add single or double consonants to spell the words correctly.

1 **c m** re c o mm end a cc o mm odate

2 **r s** emba rr a ss ha r a ss ed

3 **c s** ne c e ss ary a cc e ss ory

Complete the word sum.

4 **global** **+ ise** **+ ation** = globalisation

5 civil + ise + ation = **civilisation**

6 Roman + ise + ation = **Romanisation**

> **PART B Focus**
> **1–3:** tricky spellings; single and double consonants
> **4–6:** word structure
> **7–10:** meaning of words in different contexts

Write a definition of the word in bold.

7 a **brief** visit
   brief: lasting only a short time

8 a design **brief**
   brief: instructions about a task

9 a **current** news story
   current: relating to today

10 an electric **current**
   current: flow; movement

C Sentence work

Complete the subordinate clause using the subjunctive form. Then add a main clause.

1 If time travel were **possible,** I would travel back to Ancient Egypt.

2 If I were **head teacher,** I would allow more time for sports and PE.

3 If the council were **to ban cars in the town centre,** it would ease traffic congestion.

4 What is the purpose of sentences like these? They suggest imaginary situations.

Rewrite the sentence so that it sounds more formal.

> **PART C Focus**
> **1–4:** the subjunctive
> **5–7:** formal language and structures
> **8–10:** use of commas and a single dash for effect

5 Sorry if the building work caused you problems.
   We apologise for any inconvenience caused by the construction work.

6 You can't use your camera. The use of cameras is not permitted.

7 Be sure to have all your papers with you.
   Please ensure that you have all the relevant documentation available.

Punctuate and continue the book blurb.

8 When Lenny the alien joins Class 6, strange things happen – especially to the teacher!

9 One stormy night, Josh finds shelter in a deserted barn – but is it really deserted?

10 Marcie, an orphan, lives with her gran in Victorian London, where she is very happy –
   until her gran dies and she becomes homeless.

A Warm-up

Continue the sentence.

1. If you were to stand in the rain, *you may catch a cold.*

2. If I were prime minister, *I would make every Friday a holiday.*

3. If it were dark all day, *everyone would stay in bed.*

Draw a line to join the dinosaur name to its meaning.

4. megalosaurus — three-horned face
5. triceratops — fast plunderer
6. velociraptor — great lizard

Write the meaning of the word.
You can use a dictionary to help you.

7. **catastrophe** *a terrible event*
8. **haggard** *looking tired or ill*
9. **collaborate** *to work together*
10. **consternation** *a feeling of worry*

PART A Focus
1–3: forming sentences that use the subjunctive
4–6: word derivation and roots
7–10: word meanings; using a dictionary

B Word work

Cross out the words that are wrongly spelt.
Write the correct spellings.

1. The ~~secretry~~ ~~re-signed~~ from the ~~commitee~~.
   secretary, resigned, committee

2. The ~~professer~~ will ~~re-search~~ it ~~thoroghly~~.
   professor, research, thoroughly

3. The ~~veicles~~ were ~~queing~~ to ~~reenter~~.
   vehicles, queuing, re-enter

PART B Focus
1–3: proofreading: correcting spellings and use of hyphens
4–6: rules for adding suffixes; exceptions
7–10: word meanings in different contexts

Add the same suffix to all three words.

ous ity ify

4. sign *ify*   mod *ify*   cert *ify*
5. hazard *ous*   poison *ous* envy *ious*
6. curious *ity* generous *ity* possible *ity*

Write different definitions of each word.

7. **font** (in RE) *vessel for baptisms*
8. **font** (in IT) *style of print*
9. **colon** (in science) *part of the digestive system*
10. **colon** (in literacy) *punctuation mark*

C Sentence work

Rewrite the sentence twice. First make it shorter and more effective. Then make it longer and more effective.

Then they saw that Nina had vanished.

1. **shorter** *Nina had vanished!*

2. **longer** *As the mist cleared, they saw to their amazement that Nina had vanished.*

Complete the more formal version of these sentences using the subjunctive form.

I hope Jade improves her spelling.   **I hope Jason joins the gymnastics club.**

3. It is important that Jade *pay more attention to her spelling.*

4. I propose that Jason *become a member of the gymnastics club.*

5. Name the punctuation mark used at the end of this sentence.

   Peace returned to the planet – for a little while ... *an ellipsis*

6. Why has it been used? *To show that the peace didn't last.*

PART C Focus
1–2: editing and improving sentences
3–4: formal structures; use of the subjunctive
5–6: use of an ellipsis
7–10: commas; use of a semi-colon

Add a comma or a semi-colon.

7. The crowd parted; he stood alone.

8. As the fog lifted, dawn began to break.

9. Racing past, she grabbed the sword.

10. It was frosty; I was glad of the hot drink.

X DEFINITIVE ANSWER   X SAMPLE ANSWER

A Warm-up

Write a sentence using personification.

1. The volcano *belched out flames in fury.*
2. Frost *stroked the land with icy fingers.*
3. The machine *creaked reluctantly to life.*

aqua auto hyper
mega scope scribe vision

> **PART A Focus**
> **1–3:** personification
> **4–7:** meaning of word roots
> **8–10:** spelling strategies; related words

Make up four new words, using these roots and prefixes only. Then write a definition of each word.

4. *hypervision* — *beyond normal vision*
5. *autoscribe* — *to write automatically without thinking*
6. *megascope* — *instrument for viewing large objects*
7. *aquavision* — *the ability to see under water*

Write a related word with a different ending.

8. **vegetable** — *vegetarian*
9. **devious** — *deviate*
10. **community** — *communication*

B Word work

Use a dictionary to write the correct spelling.

1. kaleidescope — *kaleidoscope*
2. manoovre — *manoeuvre*
3. budgarigar — *budgerigar*
4. parralellogram — *parallelogram*

Write the word to go with the definition. Use the root in **bold** to help you spell it.

5. *signature* (noun)
   the way you **sign** your name

6. *sufficient* (adjective)
   it will **suffice**

> **PART B Focus**
> **1–4:** using a dictionary to check spellings
> **5–7:** using root words to help with spelling
> **8–10:** older vocabulary

7. *extraordinary* (adjective)
   out of the **ordinary**

These sentences are about a dance. Underline the words we do **not** use today. Write the words that we would use instead.

8. She <u>doth</u> but very softly go. — *does*
9. <u>Tis</u> not fast; <u>tis</u> not slow. — *It is*
10. <u>Foot</u> it <u>featly</u> here and there. — *dance, neatly*

C Sentence work

We need money to keep the animal shelter open.

Complete the next three sentences to develop this idea.

1. This means *that we need your help to raise vital funds.*
2. If *we can raise a thousand pounds, we will be able to save the shelter.*
3. On the other hand, *if we do not raise the money, the shelter will have to close.*

> **PART C Focus**
> **1–3:** text cohesion
> **4–7:** choosing grammar and vocabulary for effect
> **8–10:** correcting punctuation

Rewrite the sentence so the character's actions show their feelings. Use a progressive verb form in the sentence.

4. **Mum was angry.** *Mum was slamming the cupboard doors and clattering the pans.*
5. **Bimla was scared.** *Bimla's hands were shaking as she lifted the latch.*
6. **Oliver was sad.** *Oliver's bottom lip was quivering as he opened the letter.*
7. **Mr Jacks was happy.** *Mr Jacks was standing at the front of the class, beaming.*

Correct the punctuation in the sentence.

8. It seems that banana's are the UK's favourite fruit, we eat more of them than any other fruit.
9. Of course, keeping fit, is not just for players of sport; fitness is a goal for all.
10. There, hidden, below, was the treasure—it was just what Jo had always dreamt of.

Remind the pupil to complete Section 3 of the Progress chart on page 46 of the pupil book.

X DEFINITIVE ANSWER   X SAMPLE ANSWER

Writing task assessment sheet: Proposed road development

Name: _____   Class/Set: _____

Teacher's name: _____   Date: _____

Sentence structure and punctuation

	Always/often	Sometimes	Never
Sentences are varied in length, using main and subordinate clauses including relative clauses			
Parenthesis is used for economy of expression			
Passive voice is used to maintain or change focus			
A range of conjunctions and relative pronouns is used			
Expanded noun phrases are used to convey information concisely			
Sentences are ordered for effect (e.g. moving adverbials)			
A variety of time references are used, including the perfect form			
Modal verbs and adverbs are used to suggest possibility			
Sentences are demarcated accurately			
Commas are used to mark boundaries, clarify meaning and avoid ambiguity			
Commas, brackets and dashes are used for parenthesis			
Sophisticated punctuation marks are used (e.g. colon, semi-colon)			

Composition and effect

Features of a formal notice are used (e.g. heading, opening statement, details of meeting)			
Paragraphs have a clear focus and develop ideas			
Cohesive devices show relationship within/between paragraphs			
Grammar choices help maintain formal, balanced viewpoint (third person, generalised references)			
Appropriate choice of formal language			

Spelling

Knowledge of spelling patterns is applied correctly			
Correct spelling of words that are often misspelt			
Homophones and words that are often confused are correct			
Words with silent letters are correct			
Knowledge of word structure and word origin is used, with roots, prefixes and suffixes spelt correctly			
Rules for adding suffixes are applied and exceptions are correct			
A dictionary is used to check spellings if appropriate			

Completed proofreading task: Alone in a crowd

Name: _____   Class/Set: _____

Teacher's name: _____   Date: _____

It was incredable. one minute I was in the librery, thumming through a old
[i above incredable→incredible, O above one, a above librery→library, b above thumming, u above throogh→through, n inserted above "a old"→an]

history book on victorian britain, and now... well, now where exactly was I.?
[V above victorian, B above britain, x? after I]

The bookshelves, computers and even the building had disapeared. everything
[p inserted in disapeared→disappeared, E above everything]

had altered; I was in a street that I didnt recagnise.
[e above altared→altered, x; mark, apostrophe in didn't, o above recagnise→recognise]

Nerveously, I shrank into the shadows, consious that people were eying me
[removed e from Nerveously→Nervously, c inserted in consious→conscious, e above eying→eyeing]

with a mixcher of curiousity and suspition. I have to admit, my cloths did
[ture above mixcher→mixture, removed u from curiousity→curiosity, c above suspition→suspicion, x mark, h above cloths→clothes]

look a little out of place. everyone else was dressed like caracters in a seen
[x mark, E above everyone, h above caracters→characters, scene above seen]

from 'Oliver Twist'— all bussles and magisions hats. Was this someones humourous
[t above bussles→bustles, cians' above magisions→magicians', apostrophe in someone's, removed u from humourous→humorous]

little joke.? there must be a simple explaination.
[x mark, T above there→There, explaination→explanation]

For the moment, I felt abandonned and was desparate to find something—or
[removed n from abandonned→abandoned, e above desparate→desperate]

someone—familier. in my confussion, I set off blindly, only narrowly avoiding
[a above familier→familiar, x mark, I above in→In, removed s from confussion→confusion]

a collission with a barrow and it's owner.
[removed s from collission→collision, it's→its]

"Watch where yer goin, mate," the barrow boy exclaimed. "Just arrived from
[you're above yer, g above goin→going, ^ mark]

the country, have you.?"
[country→country, x? mark after you]

Section 3 tasks summary

_____

Full list of Schofield & Sims English Skills books

Pupil books

English Skills Introductory Book	ISBN 978 07217 1402 8
English Skills 1	ISBN 978 07217 1404 2
English Skills 2	ISBN 978 07217 1406 6
English Skills 3	ISBN 978 07217 1408 0
English Skills 4	ISBN 978 07217 1410 3
English Skills 5	ISBN 978 07217 1412 7
English Skills 6	ISBN 978 07217 1414 1

Answer books

English Skills Introductory Book Answers	ISBN 978 07217 1403 5
English Skills 1 Answers	ISBN 978 07217 1405 9
English Skills 2 Answers	ISBN 978 07217 1407 3
English Skills 3 Answers	ISBN 978 07217 1409 7
English Skills 4 Answers	ISBN 978 07217 1411 0
English Skills 5 Answers	ISBN 978 07217 1413 4
English Skills 6 Answers	ISBN 978 07217 1415 8

Teacher's Guide

The teacher's guide contains the **Entry tests**, **Diagnostic checks** and many other useful items suitable for use with the **English Skills** pupil books:

English Skills Teacher's Guide	ISBN 978 07217 1416 5

Also available

Mental Arithmetic is similar in format to **English Skills**, providing intensive maths practice.

For further information about both series, visit the Schofield & Sims website (www.schofieldandsims.co.uk).

Free downloads

A range of free downloads is available on the Schofield & Sims website, including:

- **National Curriculum chart**
- **Entry tests**
- **Entry test group record sheet**
- **Entry test marking keys**
- **Selecting the appropriate pupil book**
- **Achievement award certificates.**